The Love Language:

How to Speak Your Partner's Love Language and Build a Deeper Connection

by Sergio Rijo

Sergio Rijo

THE LOVE LANGUAGE

How to Speak Your Partner's Love Language and Build a Deeper Connection

THE LOVE LANGUAGE: HOW TO SPEAK YOUR PARTNER'S LOVE LANGUAGE AND BUILD A DEEPER CONNECTION

First edition. September 12, 2023.

Copyright © 2023 SERGIO RIJO.

ISBN: 979-8223321293

Written by SERGIO RIJO.

Table of Contents

Chapter 1: Introduction

Hello there, dear reader! Welcome to the world of love and relationships, a journey that is both thrilling and sometimes a little perplexing. In this book, we're going to dive deep into one of the most crucial aspects of any romantic relationship: the love language.

What is the Love Language?

Now, you might be wondering, what exactly is a love language? It's not a language in the traditional sense, like English or Spanish, but it's a language that speaks volumes in the realm of love and affection. Dr. Gary Chapman, a renowned marriage counselor and author, introduced the concept of love languages in his book "The Five Love Languages." According to Dr. Chapman, each person has a primary way of expressing and receiving love, which he termed their "love language."

In essence, your love language is how you prefer to give and receive love, and it can vary from person to person. There are five primary love languages, and they are:

Words of Affirmation: For some people, hearing words of love and affirmation is essential. Compliments, words of encouragement, and verbal expressions of love fill their emotional tanks.

Acts of Service: Some folks feel most loved when their partner takes action to help or support them. It could be as simple as doing the dishes, running errands, or performing other tasks that alleviate their burdens.

Receiving Gifts: There are those who treasure physical symbols of love. These can be small tokens of affection or more extravagant gifts; it's the thought and effort that count.

Quality Time: For some, nothing beats spending quality time together. Whether it's a quiet evening at home, a romantic dinner, or an adventurous day out, undivided attention is their love language.

Physical Touch: Physical touch, including hugs, kisses, and cuddles, is the primary way some people feel loved and connected.

Each of us has a dominant love language, and understanding your partner's and your own can significantly improve your relationship. Think of it as learning to speak your partner's emotional dialect.

Why is it Important to Learn Your Partner's Love Language?

Now, you might be wondering why it's so crucial to crack the code of your partner's love language. The answer lies in the foundation of any successful relationship: communication. Understanding and speaking your partner's love language is like unlocking the secret to their heart. Here are a few reasons why it's vital:

Enhanced Connection: When you speak your partner's love language, you create a deeper and more profound connection. It's like having a secret handshake that only the two of you share.

Reduced Misunderstandings: Ever had a moment when you felt unappreciated because your partner didn't react the way you expected? Learning their love language can help you avoid such misunderstandings and disappointments.

Improved Intimacy: Intimacy isn't just about physical affection. Emotional intimacy plays a massive role in a healthy relationship, and speaking your partner's love language is a surefire way to nurture it.

Strengthened Bond: The more you understand and cater to your partner's emotional needs, the stronger your bond becomes. It's like weaving an unbreakable thread of love between you two.

Conflict Resolution: When disagreements arise, knowing your partner's love language can help you navigate the storm. You'll have a better understanding of how to make amends and reconnect.

Long-Term Happiness: Ultimately, speaking your partner's love language contributes to long-term relationship satisfaction. When both partners feel loved and appreciated, the relationship is more likely to thrive.

How Can You Speak Your Partner's Love Language?

Now that you understand why learning your partner's love language is essential, let's dive into the practical aspects of how to do it. Remember, it's not about memorizing a set of rules; it's about genuine care and understanding. Here's how you can start:

Communicate Openly: The first step in learning your partner's love language is having an open and honest conversation about it. Ask them how they feel most loved and how they prefer to express their affection. Share your own love language too. This sets the stage for mutual understanding.

Observe Their Actions: Pay close attention to how your partner expresses love. Are they always offering to help with chores (Acts of Service)? Do they love cuddling on the couch (Physical Touch)? Are they constantly giving you small gifts (Receiving Gifts)? Their actions often reveal their love language.

Listen Actively: When your partner talks about their day or their feelings, listen attentively. Sometimes, their words will give you clues about what makes them feel loved. If they mention feeling appreciated when you compliment them, that's a sign of Words of Affirmation being their love language.

Experiment and Adjust: Don't be afraid to try different ways of expressing love. Sometimes, it takes a bit of trial and error to figure out what resonates most with your partner. Be open to their feedback and adjust your approach accordingly.

Quality Time: If Quality Time is their love language, make an effort to spend quality time together regularly. Plan date nights, engage in meaningful conversations, and be present in the moment. Put away your devices and give them your full attention.

Physical Touch: For those who thrive on physical touch, make an effort to initiate physical contact. This can be as simple as holding hands, hugging, or kissing. Physical touch is a powerful way to convey love and affection.

Words of Affirmation: If your partner's love language is Words of Affirmation, express your love through words. Leave them sweet notes, send loving texts, and regularly vocalize your appreciation for them.

Acts of Service: If Acts of Service is their love language, show your love by doing things for them. Help with chores, cook their favorite meal, or take care of tasks that they find burdensome.

Receiving Gifts: When it comes to Receiving Gifts, remember that it's the thought that counts. Surprise your partner with meaningful gifts that show you've been thinking about them. It doesn't have to be extravagant; it just needs to be thoughtful.

Consistency is Key: Speaking your partner's love language is not a one-time effort. It's a continuous journey of showing love and affection in a way that resonates with them. Consistency is key to maintaining a healthy and loving relationship.

Seek Feedback: Periodically check in with your partner to see how you're doing in speaking their love language. Ask if there are things you can improve or if there are specific actions that make them feel most loved.

Be Patient and Understanding: Learning and adapting to your partner's love language may take time. Be patient with yourself and your partner as you both navigate this journey together. Remember that your efforts to speak their love language are an expression of your love and commitment.

Understanding and speaking your partner's love language is a powerful way to nurture and strengthen your relationship. It's like having a secret code to unlock the door to their heart. As you embark on this journey of love and discovery, keep in mind that it's the effort and sincerity that matter most. So, go ahead, speak their love language, and watch your relationship flourish like never before. Love is a language worth learning, and the rewards are immeasurable.

Chapter 2: The Five Love Languages

Welcome back, dear reader! In this chapter, we're going to explore the fascinating world of the five love languages. These love languages, as coined by Dr. Gary Chapman, are the key to understanding how we express and receive love. Think of them as the building blocks of emotional connection in your relationship. So, grab a cozy spot, maybe a cup of your favorite beverage, and let's delve into the five love languages.

Words of Affirmation

Imagine this: Your partner whispers sweet nothings in your ear, tells you how much they love you, and appreciates you for the little things you do. If this makes your heart swell with warmth, then your primary love language might just be Words of Affirmation.

What Are Words of Affirmation?

Words of Affirmation are all about using verbal expressions to communicate love, appreciation, and affection. It's the language of compliments, encouragement, and heartfelt declarations. For those who resonate with this love language, hearing "I love you," "You mean the world to me," or "You're amazing" can be incredibly meaningful and comforting.

Why Words of Affirmation Matter

Validation: Words of Affirmation validate your feelings and reassure you that you're loved and valued. They provide a sense of security in your relationship.

Boosted Self-Esteem: Regular compliments and affirmations can boost your self-esteem and make you feel more confident and appreciated.

Emotional Connection: Expressing love through words deepens emotional connection. It shows that your partner cares enough to articulate their feelings.

Conflict Resolution: In times of conflict, using Words of Affirmation can help ease tensions and remind you both of the love that underlies any disagreements.

Daily Encouragement: These words serve as daily encouragement and can help you tackle life's challenges with greater confidence.

How to Speak the Words of Affirmation Love Language

Compliments: Make a habit of complimenting your partner genuinely. Notice their efforts and highlight their qualities.

Express Your Feelings: Don't hesitate to say "I love you" regularly. Share your feelings openly and honestly.

Encouragement: Offer words of encouragement when your partner faces difficulties or is pursuing their goals. Be their biggest cheerleader.

Appreciation: Show appreciation for the little things your partner does. A simple "thank you" can go a long way.

Surprise Notes: Leave surprise love notes or texts expressing your affection and appreciation.

Acts of Service

Picture this: Your partner wakes up early to make you breakfast, fixes your car without you asking, or takes care of chores when you're feeling overwhelmed. If these actions make you feel incredibly loved, then Acts of Service might just be your love language.

What Are Acts of Service?

Acts of Service revolve around doing things for your partner that make their life easier or more enjoyable. It's all about actions speaking louder than words. Whether it's making them a cup of tea when they're tired, taking care of household responsibilities, or helping with tasks, these actions convey love and care.

Why Acts of Service Matter

Selflessness: Acts of Service demonstrate selflessness and a willingness to prioritize your partner's well-being.

Physical Expression: They provide tangible proof of your love, making it easy for your partner to see and feel your affection.

Reduced Stress: Acts of Service can reduce your partner's stress and make them feel supported and cherished.

Emotional Connection: These actions foster emotional intimacy and create a strong bond between partners.

Effort and Thoughtfulness: They show that you're willing to put in effort and thought into making your partner's life better.

How to Speak the Acts of Service Love Language

Pay Attention: Observe what tasks or chores your partner dislikes and take the initiative to do them.

Help without Asking: Anticipate your partner's needs and offer your assistance without waiting for them to ask.

Surprise Gestures: Surprise your partner with acts of service, like cooking their favorite meal or taking care of responsibilities they usually handle.

Teamwork: Approach tasks as a team. Collaborate on projects or responsibilities, and share the load.

Express Love through Actions: Let your actions speak your love. The effort you put into making their life easier communicates your affection.

Receiving Gifts

Imagine this: Your partner surprises you with a small, thoughtful gift just because, and it brings tears of joy to your eyes. If such gestures fill your heart with happiness, then Receiving Gifts might be your love language.

What Are Receiving Gifts?

Receiving Gifts is all about the love and thoughtfulness behind a physical present. It's not about the monetary value; it's about the sentiment and effort put into selecting and giving the gift. For those who resonate with this love language, receiving gifts is a powerful way to feel loved and cherished.

Why Receiving Gifts Matter

Thoughtfulness: Receiving a gift shows that your partner has thought about you and your preferences.

Symbol of Love: Gifts serve as tangible symbols of love and affection, reminding you of your partner's feelings.

Special Occasions: They make special occasions even more memorable and meaningful.

Surprises: Surprise gifts can brighten your day and bring unexpected joy.

Investment: Giving and receiving gifts is an investment in the relationship, reflecting your commitment and care.

How to Speak the Receiving Gifts Love Language

Listen Closely: Pay attention to your partner's hints, preferences, and interests. This will help you select more meaningful gifts.

Occasional Surprises: Surprise your partner with gifts on occasions like birthdays, anniversaries, or just on a random day to express your love.

Personal Touch: Personalize your gifts to make them more meaningful. Consider their hobbies, interests, and sentimental value.

Handwritten Notes: Accompany gifts with handwritten notes expressing your feelings and why you chose that particular gift.

Quality Over Quantity: It's not about the number of gifts but the thought and meaning behind them.

Quality Time

Envision this: You and your partner spend an entire weekend together, just the two of you, without any distractions. You talk, laugh, and simply enjoy each other's company. If this scenario fills your heart with contentment, then Quality Time might be your love language.

What Is Quality Time?

Quality Time is all about giving your undivided attention to your partner and being fully present in the moment. It's not about being physically present while your mind is elsewhere; it's about engaging in meaningful interactions, deep conversations, and shared experiences.

Why Quality Time Matters

Emotional Connection: Quality Time fosters emotional intimacy and strengthens your connection with your partner.

Feeling Valued: It makes you feel valued and prioritized when your partner sets aside time just for you.

Building Memories: Shared experiences and quality moments create beautiful memories that last a lifetime.

Communication: Quality Time provides an opportunity for open and meaningful conversations, enhancing communication in your relationship.

Rejuvenation: It's a chance to recharge and rejuvenate your relationship, especially in today's fast-paced world.

How to Speak the Quality Time Love Language

Unplug: Put away your devices and minimize distractions when spending quality time with your partner.

Plan Dates: Plan regular date nights or activities that you both enjoy. It could be a movie night, a hike, or even cooking together.

Active Listening: When your partner speaks, listen actively and show that you value their thoughts and feelings.

Quality Conversations: Engage in meaningful conversations. Ask open-ended questions and share your thoughts and feelings.

Create Rituals: Establish special rituals or traditions that are unique to your relationship. These can be as simple as a Sunday morning breakfast together or a weekly game night.

Physical Touch

Imagine this: A hug from your partner makes all your worries melt away, a hand on your shoulder reassures you, and a loving kiss on the forehead makes your heart skip a beat. If physical gestures like these make you feel loved and connected, then Physical Touch might be your love language.

What Is Physical Touch?

Physical Touch is all about the power of physical connection. It includes hugs, kisses, cuddling, holding hands, and any other physical gestures that convey love and affection. For those who resonate with this love language, physical contact is an essential aspect of feeling loved and connected.

Why Physical Touch Matters

Intimacy: Physical Touch fosters a sense of emotional and physical intimacy in your relationship.

Security: It provides a sense of security and comfort, especially during challenging times.

Expression of Love: Physical gestures are a powerful way to express love and affection when words fall short.

Stress Reduction: Physical touch has been shown to reduce stress and increase feelings of well-being.

Bonding: It helps in bonding with your partner and creating a strong, physical connection.

How to Speak the Physical Touch Love Language

Frequent Affection: Offer physical affection regularly, whether it's a hug, a kiss, or simply holding hands.

Non-Sexual Touch: Remember that Physical Touch isn't limited to sexual intimacy. Non-sexual touch is equally important in conveying love and affection.

Physical Presence: Be physically present for your partner when they need it. Sometimes, a reassuring touch can say more than words.

Learn Their Preferences: Everyone has different preferences when it comes to physical touch. Learn what your partner likes and dislikes and respect their boundaries.

Cuddling: Make time for cuddling. Whether it's on the couch while watching a movie or in bed before sleep, cuddling can be incredibly comforting.

Understanding the five love languages—Words of Affirmation, Acts of Service, Receiving Gifts, Quality Time, and Physical Touch—is like discovering the secret code to your partner's heart. It's about learning how they express and receive love, and by speaking their love language, you can create a relationship that's rich in affection, understanding, and connection. So, go ahead, explore these love languages with your partner, and watch your love story unfold in the most beautiful way.

Chapter 3: Understanding Your Own Love Language

Hey there, dear reader! In this chapter, we're embarking on a journey of self-discovery—a journey that will help you unravel the mysteries of your own love language. Understanding your love language is the key to unlocking a whole new level of self-awareness and improved relationships. So, let's dive in and explore the steps to understand your unique way of giving and receiving love.

Take the Love Language Quiz

Imagine this: You're sitting on your cozy couch, sipping your favorite beverage, and you're about to embark on a journey of self-discovery. All you need is your computer or smartphone and an internet connection. It's time to take the Love Language Quiz!

What is the Love Language Quiz?

The Love Language Quiz, based on Dr. Gary Chapman's groundbreaking work, is a simple yet powerful tool to help you identify your primary love language. It's a series of questions designed to reveal how you instinctively express and receive love. By answering these questions honestly, you'll gain valuable insights into your love language.

Why Take the Quiz?

Self-Awareness: The quiz provides a structured way to reflect on your preferences and tendencies in relationships, fostering self-awareness.

Improved Relationships: Understanding your love language helps you communicate your needs and desires more effectively to your partner, leading to healthier and more fulfilling relationships.

Personal Growth: Discovering your love language can be a step toward personal growth and self-improvement. It's an opportunity to learn more about yourself and your emotional needs.

Better Relationship Choices: Armed with knowledge about your love language, you can make more informed decisions in your future relationships, choosing partners who are more compatible with your emotional needs.

How to Take the Love Language Quiz

Find a Quiet Space: Choose a quiet and comfortable space where you can focus without distractions.

Access the Quiz: Open your web browser and search for "Love Language Quiz" or visit Dr. Gary Chapman's official website, where you can find the quiz.

Answer Honestly: As you go through the quiz, answer each question honestly. Don't overthink it; go with your gut feeling.

Review Your Results: Once you've completed the quiz, review your results. The quiz will reveal your primary love language and may indicate your secondary love language as well.

Reflect on Your Love Language: Take some time to reflect on what your love language means to you. Think about past experiences in relationships and how your love language played a role.

Share with Your Partner: If you're in a relationship, consider sharing your quiz results with your partner. This can be a valuable conversation starter and lead to a deeper understanding of each other's needs.

Reflect on Your Past Relationships

Now that you've taken the Love Language Quiz and have a better understanding of your primary love language, let's take a trip down memory lane. It's time to reflect on your past relationships—both the good and the not-so-good—and see how your love language played a role.

How Did Your Love Language Influence Your Past Relationships?

Positive Experiences: Think about moments in your past relationships when your love language was fulfilled. What made those moments special, and how did they contribute to the overall happiness of the relationship?

Challenges: On the flip side, consider times when your love language wasn't understood or met. How did this affect your relationship? Were there misunderstandings or conflicts that arose due to unmet needs?

Patterns: Do you notice any patterns in your past relationships related to your love language? For example, did you consistently seek certain types of affection or appreciation?

Lessons Learned: Reflect on what you've learned from your past relationships in the context of your love language. Are there any insights or realizations that stand out?

Talk to Your Partner About Your Love Language

Now that you've gained a deeper understanding of your own love language, it's time to open up and share this insight with your partner. This conversation can be a game-changer in your relationship, as it paves the way for more effective communication and connection.

Why Share Your Love Language with Your Partner?

Enhanced Understanding: Sharing your love language with your partner helps them understand how you feel loved and appreciated.

Improved Communication: It fosters better communication by giving your partner insight into your emotional needs and preferences.

Deeper Connection: When your partner knows your love language, they can express their love in ways that resonate with you, deepening your emotional connection.

Conflict Resolution: Understanding each other's love languages can help in resolving conflicts and preventing misunderstandings.

How to Share Your Love Language with Your Partner

Choose the Right Time: Find a comfortable and relaxed moment to have this conversation. Avoid discussing it during an argument or when either of you is stressed.

Express Your Love Language: Share your primary love language with your partner and briefly explain what it means to you. Use "I" statements to convey your feelings and needs.

Provide Examples: Give specific examples of actions or gestures that align with your love language. This can help your partner understand how to fulfill your emotional needs.

Encourage Openness: Encourage your partner to share their love language as well, if they haven't already. This creates a two-way street of understanding in your relationship.

Listen Actively: Be attentive and receptive when your partner shares their love language. Ask questions and show interest in learning how to meet their emotional needs.

Plan Together: Discuss how you both can incorporate each other's love languages into your daily lives. This might involve brainstorming ideas or setting intentions for your relationship.

Be Patient and Flexible: Remember that learning to speak each other's love languages is a process. Be patient with each other as you navigate this journey of understanding and growth.

Understanding your own love language is like discovering the unique code to your heart—a code that holds the key to feeling loved, appreciated, and fulfilled in your relationships. By taking the Love Language Quiz, reflecting on your past experiences, and sharing your love language with your partner, you're taking significant steps toward creating deeper, more meaningful connections in your life. So, embrace the journey of self-discovery and watch your relationships transform in beautiful ways.

Chapter 4: Learning Your Partner's Love Language

Welcome back, dear reader, to another chapter in the love language journey. By now, you've delved into the world of your own love language, gaining valuable insights into how you express and receive love. But what about your partner's love language? Understanding and speaking it is equally vital in building a strong and lasting connection. In this chapter, we'll explore how to learn your partner's love language and nurture a love that speaks directly to their heart.

Pay Attention to Their Actions

Imagine this scenario: You're sitting across from your partner at your favorite café, sharing stories from your day. As you chat, you notice the little things they do. They spontaneously hold your hand, listen intently to your words, and surprise you with a cup of your favorite tea. These actions may be subtle, but they hold the key to discovering your partner's love language.

Why Paying Attention to Their Actions Matters

Actions Speak Louder Than Words: Sometimes, your partner's love language is evident in the things they do, rather than what they say. These actions can provide valuable clues.

Observation Builds Intimacy: Paying attention to your partner's actions shows that you care about the details of their life. It fosters a sense of intimacy and connection.

Understanding Unspoken Desires: Often, people express their love language through actions without explicitly stating their preferences. By observing these actions, you can uncover their desires.

Opportunity for Reciprocity: When you learn your partner's love language through observation, you can reciprocate their gestures in a way that resonates with them.

How to Pay Attention to Your Partner's Actions

Observe Daily Interactions: Pay attention to how your partner interacts with you and others in their daily life. Note any consistent patterns in their behavior.

Notice What They Value: Observe the things your partner values and invests time and effort in. It might be spending time with family, taking care of their health, or pursuing a hobby.

Look for Non-Verbal Cues: Often, your partner's body language and non-verbal cues can reveal their love language. Notice how they react to physical touch, gifts, or quality time.

Listen Actively: When your partner talks about their day or experiences, listen actively. They may drop hints about what makes them feel loved and appreciated.

Remember Past Gestures: Reflect on the gestures and actions that have made your partner particularly happy or emotional in the past. These can provide valuable insights.

Ask Open-Ended Questions: Engage your partner in conversations about their preferences and experiences. Open-ended questions like, "What makes you feel most loved?" can encourage them to share more.

Ask Them Directly

While paying attention to your partner's actions can provide significant clues, sometimes the most direct route to understanding their love language is a heartfelt conversation. Asking them directly about their preferences and what makes them feel loved is a courageous and considerate approach.

Why Asking Them Directly Matters

Clarity: Directly asking your partner about their love language eliminates guesswork and provides clear, unambiguous insights.

Open Communication: It encourages open and honest communication in your relationship, creating a safe space for both partners to express their needs.

Demonstrates Care: Your willingness to inquire about their love language shows that you genuinely care about their emotional well-being.

Promotes Understanding: It's an opportunity for both of you to understand each other better and build a stronger emotional connection.

Prevents Assumptions: By asking directly, you prevent making assumptions about your partner's preferences, which can lead to misunderstandings.

How to Ask Your Partner Directly About Their Love Language

Choose the Right Time: Find a calm and comfortable moment to initiate this conversation. It's best to avoid discussing it during an argument or when either of you is stressed.

Express Your Intentions: Begin by expressing your love and care for your partner. Let them know that you want to understand them better to strengthen your relationship.

Ask Open-Ended Questions: Pose open-ended questions that encourage your partner to share their thoughts and feelings. For example, "How do you feel most loved?" or "What makes you feel appreciated?"

Listen Actively: As your partner shares, listen attentively without interrupting. Show empathy and understanding, even if their love language differs from yours.

Share Your Love Language: If you haven't already, share your love language with your partner. This can be a two-way conversation that deepens mutual understanding.

Be Non-Judgmental: Ensure that your partner feels safe and non-judged during this conversation. Respect their preferences, even if they differ from your own.

Be Patient and Understanding

Learning your partner's love language is a journey, and like any journey, it takes time, patience, and understanding. It's important to remember that your partner may not have instant clarity about their love language, or they may have a combination of preferences. Here's why patience and understanding are essential:

Why Patience and Understanding Matter

Exploration and Discovery: Your partner may need time to explore and discover their own love language. It's a process of self-discovery.

Evolution of Needs: People's love languages can evolve over time or in different life circumstances. Be open to the idea that their preferences may change.

Trial and Error: Finding the perfect way to express love in your partner's preferred language may involve some trial and error. Be patient as you both navigate this process.

Respect for Differences: Your partner's love language may differ from yours, and that's okay. Respect their unique preferences and expressions of love.

How to Practice Patience and Understanding

Give Them Space: Allow your partner the space and time to reflect on their feelings and preferences. Don't rush them into defining their love language.

Support Their Exploration: Encourage your partner to explore different ways of feeling loved. Be supportive as they try to identify what resonates most with them.

Adapt and Adjust: Be flexible in your approach to speaking your partner's love language. Understand that it may take some trial and error to figure out what works best for them.

Communicate Openly: Maintain open communication with your partner throughout this journey. Share your own experiences and feelings, and encourage them to do the same.

Celebrate Progress: Celebrate each step forward in understanding your partner's love language. Even small revelations are significant milestones in your relationship.

Learning your partner's love language is an act of love in itself. It's a journey of understanding, empathy, and connection. Whether you pay attention to their actions, ask them directly, or patiently explore together, the effort you put into discovering and speaking their love language is a testament to your commitment to a loving and thriving relationship. So, be brave, be patient, and be open to the beautiful adventure of discovering how to love your partner in the most meaningful way possible.

Chapter 5: Speaking Your Partner's Love Language

Hello again, dear reader! You've journeyed far in our exploration of love languages. You've discovered your own, learned about your partner's, and now, it's time to dive into the heart of it all—how to speak your partner's love language. This chapter is all about turning that newfound knowledge into action, making your relationship richer, more meaningful, and filled with love that resonates deep within your partner's heart.

Make It a Priority

Imagine this: You're a master chef, and you've just discovered the secret ingredient that makes your partner's heart sing. It's like having a secret recipe for happiness. The first step in speaking your partner's love language is to make it a top priority in your relationship. Here's why this matters:

Why Making It a Priority Matters

Enhanced Connection: Prioritizing your partner's love language deepens your emotional connection. It shows that you're invested in their happiness and well-being.

Demonstrates Love: It's a tangible way to express your love. Actions speak louder than words, and making their love language a priority is a powerful declaration of your affection.

Consistency: Consistency is key in any successful relationship. Making it a priority means consistently speaking their love language, which helps maintain a strong connection.

Prevents Neglect: Prioritizing your partner's love language prevents it from being neglected or forgotten in the hustle and bustle of daily life.

How to Make Your Partner's Love Language a Priority

Daily Intentions: Begin each day with the intention of speaking your partner's love language. Make it a conscious decision to express your love in a way that resonates with them.

Schedule Quality Time: If Quality Time is their love language, schedule regular date nights or moments of undivided attention. Block out time on your calendar just for them.

Plan Acts of Service: If Acts of Service is their love language, plan acts of kindness and assistance. Set aside time to help with tasks or chores that matter to them.

Words of Affirmation: If their love language is Words of Affirmation, make it a habit to offer compliments, encouragement, and loving words daily.

Gifts and Surprises: For those who love Receiving Gifts, incorporate thoughtful gifts and surprises into your routine. It doesn't have to be extravagant; it's the thought that counts.

Physical Touch: If Physical Touch is their love language, initiate physical contact throughout the day. A hug, a kiss, or a loving touch can go a long way.

Check-Ins: Periodically check in with your partner to see how you're doing in speaking their love language. Ask if there are specific actions or gestures they'd appreciate more.

Be Consistent

Imagine this: You plant a seed in your garden, water it once, and expect it to flourish into a beautiful flower. But you forget to water it regularly. What happens? It withers away. The same principle applies to speaking your partner's love language—consistency is key to nurturing a thriving, loving relationship.

Why Consistency Matters

Deepens Trust: Consistency builds trust in your relationship. When your partner knows you'll consistently meet their emotional needs, they feel secure and valued.

Emotional Connection: Regularly speaking your partner's love language strengthens the emotional bond between you. It's a continuous affirmation of your love.

Predictability: Consistency creates a predictable pattern of love and affection in your relationship. Your partner can rely on your gestures of love.

Conflict Resolution: When conflicts arise, the consistency of love languages can serve as a bridge to resolution. It reminds both partners of their deep connection and love for each other.

Long-Term Happiness: Consistently speaking your partner's love language contributes to long-term relationship satisfaction and happiness.

How to Be Consistent in Speaking Your Partner's Love Language

Daily Habits: Make love language expressions a part of your daily routine. Small, consistent gestures can have a profound impact.

Set Reminders: If you're prone to forgetting, set reminders on your phone or write down your intentions in a visible place.

Learn and Adapt: Continuously learn and adapt to your partner's changing preferences. Their love language may evolve over time.

Celebrate Milestones: Celebrate milestones and special occasions in a way that aligns with your partner's love language.

Communication: Maintain open communication with your partner about their needs and whether you're meeting them consistently.

Practice Patience: Be patient with yourself and your partner as you work on consistency. It's a journey, and occasional slip-ups are natural.

Be Creative

Now, let's add a touch of creativity to your love language expressions. Think of it as adding a sprinkle of spice to your favorite dish—it elevates the experience and makes it even more memorable. Creativity injects a sense of excitement and novelty into your love language expressions.

Why Being Creative Matters

Keeps the Spark Alive: Creativity keeps the spark alive in your relationship. It prevents love language expressions from becoming routine or predictable.

Memorable Moments: Creative gestures create memorable moments that both you and your partner will cherish.

Surprise and Delight: Surprise is a potent ingredient in romance. Creative expressions of love language can surprise and delight your partner.

Adaptability: Creativity allows you to adapt your love language expressions to different situations and occasions, keeping your relationship dynamic.

Personal Touch: Creative expressions are often more personalized and tailored to your partner's unique preferences.

How to Be Creative in Speaking Your Partner's Love Language

Thoughtful Surprises: Plan surprise gestures that align with your partner's love language. It could be a surprise date night for Quality Time lovers or a heartfelt love letter for Words of Affirmation enthusiasts.

Incorporate Interests: Consider your partner's hobbies and interests when planning creative expressions of love. It shows that you're attentive and genuinely care.

Experiment and Explore: Don't be afraid to try new things and experiment with different ways of expressing their love language.

Use Your Imagination: Let your imagination run wild. Think of unique and unexpected ways to show your love.

Collaborate: Collaborate with your partner on creative expressions. Brainstorm ideas together and make it a joint project.

Take Risks: Creativity often involves taking risks. Be willing to step out of your comfort zone to create memorable moments.

Examples of Creative Love Language Expressions

Words of Affirmation: Record a heartfelt audio message expressing your love and appreciation. Play it for your partner when they least expect it.

Acts of Service: Create a "coupon book" of acts of service you're willing to do for your partner, such as cooking their favorite meal or handling their chores.

Receiving Gifts: Give your partner a surprise gift that's not for a special occasion—a "just because" gift that shows your love and thoughtfulness.

Quality Time: Plan a surprise adventure day, complete with clues and surprises at each stop along the way.

Physical Touch: Surprise your partner with a dance in the living room to their favorite song or a spontaneous slow dance in the kitchen.

Speaking your partner's love language is like composing a beautiful symphony of love, with each note and gesture resonating deep within their heart. By making it a priority, being consistent, and infusing creativity into your expressions, you're nurturing a relationship that's not only strong but also filled with joy, intimacy, and heartfelt connection. So, keep the flame of love burning bright, and let your creative spirit soar as you speak the language of love that your partner treasures most.

Chapter 6: Overcoming Challenges

Hello again, dear reader. As we venture further into the enchanting realm of love languages, we must address a topic that every journey faces—challenges. While understanding and speaking your partner's love language can bring joy and fulfillment, it's not without its hurdles. In this chapter, we'll explore the common challenges that arise when love languages clash, and we'll discover the resilience and determination it takes to overcome them.

Different Love Languages Can Clash

Picture this: You and your partner are dancing to the rhythm of love, each expressing your affection in your unique way. But suddenly, you step on each other's toes. Your partner feels unloved because you're not speaking their love language, and you feel frustrated because you're not getting through to them. This clash of love languages is a scenario familiar to many couples.

Why Different Love Languages Can Clash

Miscommunication: When partners have different love languages, there's a higher chance of miscommunication. What one person considers an expression of love may not resonate with the other.

Unmet Expectations: Unmet expectations can lead to frustration and disappointment. If your partner doesn't understand your love language, you may feel like your needs are consistently unmet.

Assumptions: Assumptions about how love should be expressed can lead to misunderstandings. You might assume your partner knows what you need without explicitly stating it.

Feeling Unloved: When your love language isn't spoken, you may feel unloved or unappreciated, even though your partner may be expressing love in their own way.

Conflict Triggers: Love language clashes can become triggers for conflicts and arguments if not addressed and resolved.

How Different Love Languages Can Clash

Words of Affirmation vs. Acts of Service: If one partner's primary love language is Words of Affirmation, they may crave verbal expressions of love. If the other partner's love language is Acts of Service, they may show love by taking care of tasks. This can lead to one partner feeling neglected and unloved, while the other feels unappreciated for their efforts.

Quality Time vs. Independence: A partner who values Quality Time may seek closeness and togetherness. If the other partner values independence and personal space, they may misinterpret this need for space as rejection.

Receiving Gifts vs. Minimalism: Someone who loves Receiving Gifts may feel cherished when they receive thoughtful presents. If their partner values minimalism and doesn't place importance on physical gifts, the gift lover may feel unloved.

Physical Touch vs. Personal Space: A partner who values Physical Touch may crave constant physical contact. If their partner values personal space, they may feel suffocated and overwhelmed by the constant need for touch.

Acts of Service vs. Self-Sufficiency: A partner who values Acts of Service may appreciate help and assistance. If their partner values self-sufficiency, they may interpret this help as a lack of trust in their abilities.

It Takes Time and Effort

Now, let's delve into the heart of the matter—overcoming the challenges posed by different love languages. While it may seem daunting at times, the effort you put into understanding, empathizing, and adapting to your partner's love language is well worth it. Here's why it's crucial:

Why It Takes Time and Effort

Building Understanding: It takes time to truly understand your partner's love language, their needs, and their emotional triggers.

Changing Habits: Shifting your behavior and speaking a different love language than your own requires effort and conscious choices.

Effective Communication: It takes time to establish effective communication with your partner about your respective love languages and preferences.

Adapting to Differences: Adapting to differences and finding common ground takes patience and effort, especially when love languages clash.

Sustaining Effort: Consistency is key, and it can be challenging to sustain effort over the long term.

How to Put in the Time and Effort

Empathy: Empathize with your partner's perspective and emotional needs. Try to see the world from their point of view.

Effective Communication: Keep the lines of communication open. Discuss your love languages, express your feelings, and listen to your partner's concerns.

Learn and Adapt: Continuously learn about your partner's love language and preferences. Adapt your behavior accordingly.

Seek Guidance: If you're facing persistent challenges, consider seeking guidance from a relationship counselor or therapist who specializes in love languages.

Celebrate Progress: Celebrate small victories and moments of progress in understanding and speaking each other's love languages.

Self-Reflect: Take time to self-reflect on your own behavior and attitudes. Are there any biases or assumptions you need to address?

Practice Patience: Be patient with yourself and your partner as you navigate the complexities of love languages. Change takes time.

Don't Give Up

Imagine this: You're on a challenging hike, and the path is steep and rocky. You stumble, and your legs ache. You're tempted to turn back, but you remember the breathtaking view waiting at the summit. This journey, too, is worth the effort. Don't give up on understanding and speaking your partner's love language, even when the path is tough.

Why Not Giving Up Matters

Deepening Connection: Persisting through challenges deepens your emotional connection and strengthens your bond.

Resilience: Overcoming love language obstacles builds resilience in your relationship. It's a testament to your commitment.

Fulfillment: Speaking your partner's love language leads to greater fulfillment and satisfaction in your relationship.

Conflict Resolution: Working through love language clashes equips you with valuable conflict resolution skills.

Growing Together: The journey of understanding and adapting to your partner's love language is a form of personal and relational growth.

How to Stay Committed and Not Give Up

Remind Yourself Why: When faced with challenges, remind yourself why you're committed to understanding and speaking your partner's love language. Focus on the positive impact it has on your relationship.

Seek Support: Lean on friends, family, or a therapist for support and guidance when facing particularly challenging obstacles.

Celebrate Progress: Celebrate the progress you make, even if it's small steps forward. Acknowledge the effort you're putting into your relationship.

Stay Patient: Patience is a virtue. Remember that understanding and adapting to your partner's love language is a journey, not a destination.

Continuous Learning: Keep learning about love languages and exploring new ways to connect with your partner. Knowledge is a powerful tool in this journey.

Every love story has its challenges, and understanding and speaking your partner's love language is no exception. It's a journey of self-discovery, empathy, and adaptation. But remember, the view from the summit—the deep connection, fulfillment, and intimacy—is worth the effort. As you navigate the twists and turns of love languages, stay committed, communicate openly, and never give up on the beautiful journey of loving and being loved in the most meaningful way.

Chapter 7: Building a Deeper Connection

Hello again, dear reader. By now, you've embarked on an incredible journey of love, exploring the intricacies of love languages, overcoming challenges, and making a conscious effort to understand and speak your partner's love language. In this chapter, we'll delve into the beautiful rewards of your efforts—building a deeper connection with your partner.

When You Speak Your Partner's Love Language, You Feel Closer to Them

Picture this: You and your partner are standing on the edge of a vast, uncharted ocean. As you communicate through your love languages, it's as if you have a shared map that guides you through the waves and storms of life. Speaking your partner's love language is the compass that keeps you connected and moving forward together.

Why Speaking Your Partner's Love Language Deepens Your Connection

Shared Understanding: Speaking your partner's love language fosters a shared understanding of each other's emotional needs and desires.

Emotional Intimacy: It creates a profound sense of emotional intimacy, allowing you to connect on a deeper level.

Stronger Bond: The more you speak each other's love languages, the stronger your bond becomes. You become each other's safe haven.

Trust and Security: When you consistently speak your partner's love language, they feel a deep sense of trust and security in the relationship.

Shared Journey: It's like embarking on a shared journey of love and growth, where both partners are actively invested in each other's happiness.

How Speaking Your Partner's Love Language Deepens the Connection

Enhanced Communication: Speaking your partner's love language enhances communication. It's a form of emotional communication that goes beyond words.

Mutual Fulfillment: When both partners have their love languages spoken, they experience mutual fulfillment and satisfaction.

Conflict Resolution: It serves as a powerful tool for conflict resolution. It reminds you of your love and commitment, helping you navigate conflicts with empathy.

Shared Goals: Couples who speak each other's love languages often share similar relationship goals and priorities.

Strengthened Trust: It strengthens trust and reduces insecurity. When you consistently speak your partner's love language, they know you're dedicated to the relationship.

You Feel More Loved and Appreciated

Imagine this: Your partner surprises you with a heartfelt letter, expressing their love and appreciation in Words of Affirmation. They speak your love language fluently, and it's as if the words on that page are a warm embrace, wrapping you in love. When your partner speaks your love language, you feel more loved and appreciated than ever before.

Why Feeling More Loved and Appreciated Matters

Emotional Well-Being: Feeling loved and appreciated contributes significantly to your emotional well-being and happiness.

Confidence: It boosts your confidence and self-esteem, knowing that you're cherished and valued by your partner.

Secure Attachment: Feeling loved and appreciated creates a secure attachment in the relationship, fostering a sense of safety and trust.

Greater Satisfaction: You experience greater satisfaction and fulfillment in the relationship when your emotional needs are met.

Resilience: Feeling loved and appreciated builds resilience in the relationship, helping you both weather life's storms together.

How Feeling More Loved and Appreciated Transforms Your Relationship

Increased Affection: Partners who feel loved and appreciated are more affectionate and attentive to each other's needs.

Positive Feedback Loop: It creates a positive feedback loop of affection and appreciation. As you express love, you receive it in return, reinforcing the bond.

Lessens Insecurities: Feeling loved and appreciated reduces insecurities and jealousy in the relationship.

Greater Patience: You're more patient and understanding with each other's quirks and imperfections.

Shared Joy: Partners who feel loved and appreciated often experience more moments of shared joy and laughter.

You Have a Stronger Relationship

Now, let's bask in the beauty of it all—you have a stronger relationship. Your love languages have become a secret code that unlocks the door to a deeper, more meaningful connection. Your relationship is a fortress built on love, trust, and mutual understanding.

Why Having a Stronger Relationship Matters

Longevity: Strong relationships are more likely to stand the test of time. They're built to weather life's challenges.

Happiness: A strong relationship contributes to greater happiness and life satisfaction for both partners.

Healthy Communication: Partners in strong relationships often have healthy communication patterns, reducing conflicts and misunderstandings.

Emotional Support: A strong relationship provides a robust support system during tough times. It's the comforting presence that helps you navigate life's ups and downs.

How Having a Stronger Relationship Transforms Your Life

Enhanced Quality of Life: Your overall quality of life improves as a result of the strength of your relationship. You carry the happiness and fulfillment from your relationship into other areas of your life.

Stress Reduction: A strong relationship acts as a buffer against stress. Knowing you have a partner you can rely on reduces the burdens of daily life.

Improved Well-Being: Strong relationships are associated with better physical and mental well-being. You experience less stress, better health, and greater life satisfaction.

Sense of Belonging: Your relationship provides a profound sense of belonging and companionship. You know you have a partner who will stand by your side through thick and thin.

Shared Dreams: Partners in strong relationships often share dreams and aspirations. Your relationship becomes a journey of growth and achievement together.

How Speaking Your Partner's Love Language Strengthens Your Relationship

Open Communication: It encourages open and honest communication about your emotional needs, desires, and expectations.

Conflict Resolution: The foundation of a strong relationship built on love languages facilitates constructive conflict resolution. You approach disagreements with empathy and a shared commitment to finding solutions.

Mutual Growth: As you journey together, understanding and speaking each other's love languages lead to personal and relational growth. You evolve as individuals and as a couple.

Shared Experiences: Love language expressions create cherished memories and experiences that fortify your bond. These shared moments become the legacy of your love story.

Continual Nurturing: The strength of your relationship requires continual nurturing. Love language expressions are the water and sunlight that help your love grow and flourish.

Speaking your partner's love language isn't merely a skill; it's a journey of discovery, connection, and profound love. It's the symphony of two hearts beating in harmony, the tapestry of a love story woven with threads of closeness, appreciation, and strength. As you navigate the intricate terrain of love languages, remember that building a deeper connection, feeling more loved and appreciated, and having a stronger relationship are the rewards waiting for you. So, dear reader, embrace the power of love languages, nurture your connection, and treasure the love that blossoms when you speak your partner's unique language of love. Your journey continues, and the path ahead is filled with boundless love and possibility.

Chapter 8: Maintaining a Healthy Relationship

Hello, dear reader. As we venture into the realm of maintaining a healthy relationship, we are now well-versed in the language of love, understanding the nuances of love languages, building a profound connection, and feeling cherished and appreciated. However, the journey is far from over. In this chapter, we will delve into the art of nurturing and preserving the beautiful bond you've built, ensuring that your love story remains vibrant, resilient, and enduring.

Keep Learning About Each Other's Love Languages

Picture this: You and your partner are sitting together, reminiscing about your journey so far. You've come a long way in understanding each other's love languages, but you realize that this learning process is ongoing. Just as a garden needs care and attention to flourish, so does your relationship.

Why It's Important to Keep Learning About Love Languages

Evolution: People change over time, and so do their emotional needs. What speaks to your partner's heart today may evolve in the future.

Variability: Love languages can be multifaceted. While you may have identified the primary love language, there may be secondary or evolving languages to consider.

Depth: The more you delve into your partner's love language, the deeper your connection becomes. There's always more to discover.

Surprises: Continuing to learn about each other's love languages can lead to delightful surprises and spontaneous acts of love.

How to Keep Learning About Love Languages

Open Communication: Maintain open and honest communication about your emotional needs and love languages. Share your discoveries and evolving preferences.

Stay Curious: Be curious about your partner's changing desires and preferences. Ask questions and show genuine interest.

Revisit the Quiz: Periodically revisit the love language quiz together. It can serve as a helpful tool for self-assessment and discussion.

Explore New Ways: Be open to exploring new ways of expressing love within your partner's language. Be creative and adaptable.

Celebrate Growth: Celebrate the growth in your understanding of each other's love languages. Acknowledge the progress you've made.

Be Willing to Compromise

Imagine this: You and your partner are planning a weekend getaway. Your ideal vacation involves Quality Time—cozy evenings together, long walks, and meaningful conversations. However, your partner's primary love language is Adventure, and they envision a thrilling outdoor adventure. In this moment, compromise becomes the bridge that connects your desires and creates harmony.

Why Compromise is Vital in a Relationship

Balancing Needs: Compromise allows you to balance both partners' emotional needs and desires. It's the key to finding middle ground.

Flexibility: Life is full of unexpected twists and turns. Compromise teaches flexibility and adaptability.

Conflict Resolution: Many conflicts in relationships arise from differences in needs and preferences. Compromise is a powerful conflict resolution tool.

Growth: Learning to compromise fosters personal growth and strengthens your relationship. It's a testament to your commitment to each other's happiness.

How to Practice Compromise

Communication: Open and respectful communication is the foundation of compromise. Discuss your desires, needs, and boundaries.

Empathy: Put yourself in your partner's shoes to better understand their perspective and motivations.

Flexibility: Be willing to adapt and find creative solutions that meet both your needs to some extent.

Prioritize: Decide what aspects of a situation are most important to each of you and focus on those.

Give and Take: Compromise often involves a give-and-take approach. You may give in on one occasion, and your partner may do the same on another.

Celebrate Compromises: Acknowledge and appreciate the compromises you both make. It's a way to reinforce their value in your relationship.

Don't Take Each Other for Granted

Close your eyes and imagine this: You're sitting in your favorite spot, surrounded by the comforting familiarity of your home. Your partner walks by, and you realize just how much their presence means to you. In the hustle and bustle of everyday life, it's easy to overlook the treasures we have. Don't let your partner be one of them.

Why Not Taking Each Other for Granted is Essential

Maintaining Appreciation: Taking each other for granted can erode appreciation over time. It's essential to maintain a sense of wonder and gratitude for your partner.

Preserving Romance: Romance flourishes when both partners continue to make efforts to impress and surprise each other.

Building Trust: Knowing that you're valued and appreciated reinforces trust and emotional safety in the relationship.

Long-Term Happiness: A sense of mutual appreciation contributes significantly to long-term happiness in a relationship.

How to Avoid Taking Each Other for Granted

Express Gratitude: Regularly express gratitude for the little things your partner does. Say "thank you" and acknowledge their efforts.

Quality Time: Spend quality time together without distractions. Give each other your full attention.

Surprise Gestures: Keep the element of surprise alive by occasionally planning unexpected gestures or surprises for your partner.

Communication: Talk openly about your feelings and appreciation for each other. Share your love and admiration.

Date Nights: Schedule regular date nights or special outings to keep the romance alive.

Remember the Beginning: Reflect on the early days of your relationship and what initially drew you to each other. Rekindle those feelings.

Avoid Complacency: Guard against complacency by continuously seeking ways to improve and grow together.

Maintaining a healthy relationship is a lifelong journey of learning, compromise, and appreciation. Just as a garden requires care and attention to thrive, your relationship needs nurturing to remain vibrant and resilient. By continuing to learn about each other's love languages, practicing compromise, and never taking each other for granted, you're ensuring that your love story remains a beautiful, evolving masterpiece. Your relationship is a testament to the enduring power of love, and its pages are filled with the stories of your growth, shared dreams, and unwavering commitment. So, dear reader, cherish your journey together, and let the love you've cultivated continue to blossom. The best chapters of your love story are yet to come.

Chapter 9: The Power of Words

Welcome, dear reader, to a chapter that delves deep into the heart of human connection. Here, we explore the immense power of words, particularly Words of Affirmation, as a potent tool for expressing love, building intimacy, and nurturing the bonds that tie us together. The words we choose can shape our relationships and touch the souls of those we love. So, let's embark on this journey into the world of spoken affection.

Words of Affirmation Can Be a Powerful Way to Show Love

Close your eyes and imagine this: You're sitting across from your partner, sharing a quiet moment. In a voice filled with sincerity and love, you say, "I appreciate everything you do for us. You are amazing, and I'm grateful to have you in my life." In that instant, the world seems to stand still, and your partner's eyes fill with tears of joy. These are the magical moments that Words of Affirmation can create.

Why Words of Affirmation Are Powerful

Verbal Affection: Words of Affirmation are a form of verbal affection. They provide reassurance, validation, and a sense of being loved and appreciated.

Emotional Connection: Expressing your feelings through words deepens the emotional connection between you and your partner.

Boosts Self-Esteem: Compliments and affirmations boost your partner's self-esteem and confidence, making them feel valued and respected.

Positive Reinforcement: Encouraging words reinforce positive behavior and strengthen the traits you admire in your partner.

Effective Communication: Words are a means of effective communication. Expressing your love verbally ensures that your message is clear and heartfelt.

How to Use Words of Affirmation Effectively

Be Sincere: Authenticity is key. Speak from the heart, and let your words reflect your true feelings.

Specific Compliments: Be specific in your compliments. Instead of saying "you're great," say "I admire how you handle challenges with grace."

Regular Affirmations: Make Words of Affirmation a regular part of your communication. Consistency reinforces their power.

Use "I" Statements: Say "I love you" instead of "you are loved." It makes your affirmation more personal.

Pay Attention: Be attentive to your partner's actions and qualities that deserve affirmation. Acknowledge their efforts and strengths.

Choose Your Words Carefully

Imagine this: You're crafting a love letter to your partner, choosing each word with care. Every word you select is like a brushstroke on a canvas, painting a picture of your love. The words you choose hold the power to evoke emotions, inspire, and create lasting memories.

Why Choosing Words Carefully Matters

Impactful Expression: Well-chosen words have a profound impact. They can touch the soul and create lasting emotional imprints.

Avoid Miscommunication: Carefully chosen words help avoid misunderstandings and misinterpretations in a relationship.

Respectful Communication: Thoughtful words show respect for your partner's feelings and opinions, fostering a healthier dialogue.

Strengthen Connection: Choosing words carefully deepens your emotional connection and demonstrates your commitment to effective communication.

How to Choose Your Words Carefully

Reflect Before Speaking: Take a moment to reflect on what you want to convey. Consider the tone and impact of your words.

Practice Empathy: Put yourself in your partner's shoes to gauge how your words might be received. Empathy enhances communication.

Use Positive Language: Frame your words in a positive and constructive manner. Avoid harsh criticism or negative language.

Clarify Intentions: If there's any room for misunderstanding, clarify your intentions. Ensure your partner understands the message you're trying to convey.

Be Mindful of Timing: Consider the timing of your words. Sometimes, waiting for the right moment can make your message more meaningful.

Make Sure They Are Meaningful

Imagine this: You and your partner are sharing a quiet evening together. In the midst of everyday conversations, you pause and say, "I just want you to know that you mean the world to me. I'm so grateful for your presence in my life." These words carry weight, significance, and depth. They are not mere utterances; they are meaningful expressions of love.

Why Meaningful Words Are Essential

Depth of Connection: Meaningful words foster a deeper connection by demonstrating the depth of your emotions and the importance of your partner in your life.

Lasting Impact: Meaningful words leave a lasting impact, creating memories and emotional bonds that endure over time.

Nurturing Love: They nurture love by reminding both partners of their value and significance in each other's hearts.

Enhanced Intimacy: Meaningful words enhance emotional intimacy by allowing partners to share their innermost thoughts and feelings.

How to Make Your Words Meaningful

Speak from the Heart: Allow your genuine emotions to guide your words. Speak with authenticity, and let your heart do the talking.

Reflect on Your Feelings: Take time to reflect on your feelings for your partner. Consider what you admire, appreciate, and love about them.

Choose Words with Care: Select words and phrases that encapsulate the depth of your feelings. Avoid clichés or empty phrases.

Use Personal Stories: Sharing personal anecdotes or stories that illustrate your feelings can make your words more meaningful.

Reiterate Your Commitment: Reinforce your commitment to the relationship through meaningful words. Let your partner know that you're in it for the long haul.

The power of words is an incredible force that can shape the landscape of your relationship. Words of Affirmation, chosen carefully and spoken meaningfully, can nurture love, deepen connections, and strengthen bonds. They are the poetry of your love story, the soundtrack of your emotions, and the bridge that connects your hearts.

So, dear reader, let your words be a testament to the love you feel, the appreciation you hold, and the commitment you share with your partner. As you navigate the seas of love, remember that your words have the power to light up the path, to soothe the storms, and to create a love story that will be cherished for a lifetime. Continue to speak the language of love with sincerity, care, and depth, and watch your relationship flourish into a beautiful and lasting masterpiece.

Chapter 10: Acts of Service

Welcome, dear reader, to a chapter that celebrates the profound impact of Acts of Service in nurturing love and strengthening the bonds of your relationship. In a world where actions often speak louder than words, these thoughtful gestures have the power to convey love, care, and devotion in the most tangible way. So, let's dive into the world of Acts of Service, where love is demonstrated through selfless deeds and thoughtful actions.

Acts of Service Can Show Your Partner That You Care

Imagine this: Your partner has had a long, exhausting day at work, and you decide to take on their chores without them asking. You prepare a warm meal, tidy up the house, and create a soothing ambiance. When your partner walks through the door and sees what you've done, their face lights up with gratitude and relief. In that moment, Acts of Service become a language of love that transcends words.

Why Acts of Service Are a Powerful Expression of Love

Visible Dedication: Acts of Service are visible manifestations of your commitment and love. They are tangible proof of your devotion.

Alleviating Burdens: These acts can ease the burdens of daily life, making your partner feel supported and cared for.

Emotional Connection: Acts of Service create a deep emotional connection by demonstrating your willingness to invest time and effort for your partner's well-being.

Strengthening Trust: Consistently following through on acts of service builds trust and reinforces the reliability of your love.

Love in Action: They are a form of love in action, where words are transformed into meaningful deeds.

How to Use Acts of Service to Show Your Love

Pay Attention: Observe your partner's needs and preferences. Be attentive to what would make their life easier or more enjoyable.

Initiate: Take the initiative to perform acts of service without waiting for your partner to ask. Anticipate their needs.

Consistency: Make acts of service a regular part of your relationship. Consistency reinforces their impact.

Variety: Offer a variety of acts of service to cater to different aspects of your partner's life, from household chores to emotional support.

Communicate: Talk openly with your partner about their preferences and the acts of service that resonate most with them.

Do Things That They Appreciate

Picture this: You're planning a surprise weekend getaway for your partner. Instead of organizing activities that you love, you choose experiences and destinations that align with their interests and preferences. The smile on their face when you reveal your thoughtful surprise is a testament to the importance of doing things that your partner truly appreciates.

Why Doing Things Your Partner Appreciates Matters

Personalized Love: Tailoring your actions to your partner's preferences demonstrates your commitment to a personalized and meaningful form of love.

Enhanced Connection: Engaging in activities your partner enjoys deepens your connection by creating shared experiences and memories.

Respect: It's a way of showing respect for your partner's individuality and unique interests.

Emotional Fulfillment: Doing things your partner appreciates can lead to a profound sense of emotional fulfillment and satisfaction.

Shared Joy: Witnessing your partner's happiness and gratitude can bring you shared moments of joy and contentment.

How to Do Things That Your Partner Appreciates

Ask and Listen: Have open conversations with your partner about their interests, passions, and preferences. Ask questions and truly listen to their responses.

Take an Interest: Make an effort to take an interest in the things that matter to your partner. Educate yourself about their hobbies or interests.

Plan Thoughtful Surprises: Surprise your partner with thoughtful gestures or experiences that align with their preferences.

Participate Actively: Engage actively in activities your partner enjoys, whether it's a hobby, a sport, or a shared interest.

Celebrate Milestones: Mark special occasions with celebrations or activities that hold meaning for your partner.

Don't Wait to Be Asked

Imagine this: Your partner is feeling overwhelmed by a busy week at work, and they could use some help with household chores. Instead of waiting for them to ask, you step in and take care of the tasks that need attention. This proactive approach is a powerful demonstration of your love and consideration.

Why Not Waiting to Be Asked Is a Sign of Love

Anticipating Needs: Taking the initiative to help without being asked shows that you're attuned to your partner's needs and emotions.

Lessening Stress: It can significantly reduce your partner's stress and workload, allowing them to relax and recharge.

Solidarity: It's a gesture of solidarity and partnership, reinforcing your commitment to facing life's challenges together.

Spontaneous Love: Acts of service performed without prompting are often seen as spontaneous acts of love, which can be deeply appreciated.

How to Proactively Show Your Love Through Acts of Service

Observation: Pay attention to your partner's cues and body language. Sometimes, their needs may not be verbalized but can be observed.

Plan Ahead: Anticipate situations or periods when your partner might need assistance or support. Plan ahead to offer your help.

Surprise Gestures: Surprise your partner with acts of service they didn't expect. It could be something as simple as making their favorite breakfast or taking care of a task on their to-do list.

Express Love: Let your actions convey your love. When you perform acts of service without being asked, they carry a message of love, care, and thoughtfulness.

Feedback: Encourage open communication with your partner about how they feel regarding your proactive acts of service. Their feedback can help you tailor your efforts.

Acts of Service are the unsung heroes of love, expressing devotion and care through selfless deeds and thoughtful actions. They are the silent promises to be there for your partner, to make their life easier, and to create moments of joy and connection. As you navigate the landscape of love, remember that the smallest acts of service can have the most significant impact. So, dear reader, let your love shine through your actions, let your partner feel your devotion through your deeds, and let Acts of Service be the bridge that connects your hearts. Your love story is a tapestry woven with threads of love, consideration, and shared experiences. As you embrace the power of Acts of Service, may your relationship continue to flourish, nurtured by the care and love that flow through your actions.

Chapter 11: Receiving Gifts

Welcome to a chapter that unwraps the significance of giving and receiving gifts in the language of love. In a world filled with tangible tokens of affection, we explore how even the simplest of presents can hold the power to connect, express emotions, and create cherished memories. Whether it's a grand gesture or a small token, let's delve into the world of Receiving Gifts and discover the joy in giving.

Gifts Don't Have to Be Expensive

Picture this: You're walking hand in hand with your partner through a quaint, charming town. You come across an artisan shop with handcrafted jewelry, and you spot a delicate silver necklace with a small heart pendant. You know it's the perfect gift. It's not extravagant, but it's a symbol of your love and thoughtfulness. In that moment, you understand that gifts don't have to come with a hefty price tag to be meaningful.

Why Gifts Don't Have to Be Expensive to Be Meaningful

Thought and Effort: The value of a gift isn't solely determined by its cost but by the thought and effort put into choosing it.

Personal Connection: A meaningful gift reflects your understanding of your partner's preferences and interests, regardless of its price.

Emotional Significance: Small, heartfelt gifts can carry deep emotional significance, creating lasting memories.

Daily Tokens of Love: Inexpensive gifts can serve as daily reminders of your love, appreciation, and thoughtfulness.

Affordability: Meaningful gifts can be accessible to everyone, irrespective of their budget.

How to Choose Thoughtful, Inexpensive Gifts

Consider Their Interests: Think about your partner's hobbies, passions, and interests. A small gift related to something they love can be incredibly meaningful.

Personalized Tokens: Opt for personalized gifts, such as a custom-made piece of artwork, a handwritten letter, or a mixtape of songs that hold sentimental value.

Symbolic Items: Look for items that hold symbolic value, like a keychain that represents a shared memory or a special place you both love.

Handmade with Love: Handmade gifts, even simple ones like baked goods or a handcrafted card, can be deeply appreciated for the effort and care they represent.

Plan Thoughtful Surprises: Sometimes, the most meaningful gifts are unexpected surprises that convey your love and affection.

The Thoughtfulness Behind the Gift Is What Matters

Imagine this: Your partner presents you with a beautifully wrapped gift box. You eagerly unwrap it to find a book, not just any book, but a special edition of your favorite childhood story. They explain that they remembered you mentioning it once, and they wanted to surprise you with a thoughtful gift. In that moment, it's not the book itself that touches your heart; it's the thought and consideration that went into choosing it.

Why the Thoughtfulness Behind the Gift Matters Most

Emotional Connection: Thoughtful gifts foster a deeper emotional connection by showing that you truly understand and care for your partner.

Meaningful Gestures: The thoughtfulness behind the gift elevates it from a mere object to a meaningful gesture of love and appreciation.

Memories: Thoughtful gifts create lasting memories of moments when you felt truly seen and loved.

Effort Matters: The effort put into choosing a gift speaks volumes about your commitment to making your partner happy.

Appreciation: Thoughtful gifts are often appreciated more than extravagant ones because they touch the heart.

How to Choose Thoughtful Gifts

Listen Actively: Pay attention to your partner's conversations and hints about things they like or need. Active listening is the key to thoughtful gift-giving.

Consider Their Personality: Think about your partner's personality traits and preferences when selecting a gift. Is it something that aligns with who they are?

Reflect on Shared Moments: Recall shared experiences and memories that have significance in your relationship. Choose gifts that reference these moments.

Be Mindful of Timing: Consider the timing of the gift. Is there a special occasion or milestone that makes the gift more meaningful?

Express Your Feelings: Include a heartfelt note or letter with the gift, expressing your love and the reasons why you chose it for your partner.

Choose Gifts That Your Partner Will Love

Close your eyes and imagine this: It's your partner's birthday, and you've been planning a surprise gift for weeks. You decide to take them on a hot air balloon ride because you know it's a dream they've always had. As you both soar above the world, taking in breathtaking views, you see the pure joy and excitement in your partner's eyes. You realize that choosing gifts your partner will love is like capturing their heart's desires and turning them into reality.

Why Choosing Gifts Your Partner Will Love Matters

Personal Connection: Selecting gifts that align with your partner's tastes and desires demonstrates a deep personal connection.

Enhanced Happiness: Gifts your partner loves bring them genuine happiness and a sense of feeling truly cherished.

Strengthening Bonds: Such gifts strengthen the bonds in your relationship by showing your commitment to their happiness.

Memorable Experiences: Experience-based gifts create lasting memories and shared adventures that you both treasure.

Appreciation: When your partner loves the gift you've chosen, it deepens their appreciation for your thoughtfulness and consideration.

How to Choose Gifts Your Partner Will Love

Ask Directly: If you're unsure, don't hesitate to ask your partner about their preferences or create a wish list together.

Observe Their Interests: Pay attention to their hobbies, interests, and collections. These can provide excellent gift ideas.

Incorporate Sentimentality: Consider incorporating sentimental elements, such as choosing gifts related to special memories or shared experiences.

Be Mindful of Their Needs: Think about practical gifts that cater to your partner's needs or solve a problem they've mentioned.

Quality Over Quantity: It's not about the number of gifts but the thought and quality behind them that matter most.

Gift-giving is a language of love, a way to express affection, appreciation, and thoughtfulness in tangible form. Whether the gifts are grand or humble, expensive or simple, their significance lies in the love, consideration, and emotions they represent. As you continue to navigate the beautiful journey of your relationship, remember that every gift you exchange is a piece of your heart offered to your partner. So, dear reader, embrace the joy of giving and receiving, let your heart guide your choices, and let your love shine through the thoughtful tokens that connect you both. Your love story is adorned with these precious moments of gifting, creating a tapestry of shared joy, appreciation, and cherished memories.

Chapter 12: Quality Time

Welcome, dear reader, to a chapter that explores the profound significance of Quality Time in the realm of love. Quality Time is not just a love language; it's a language of presence, connection, and intimacy. In a world filled with distractions, schedules, and screens, we'll delve into the art of carving out moments to truly be with your partner and nurture the bonds that define your relationship.

Quality Time Is the Most Important Love Language for Many People

Imagine this: You and your partner are sitting on a cozy couch, a warm blanket draped over your laps. The room is softly lit, and you're engrossed in a deep, heartfelt conversation. You're not just physically present; your attention and focus are entirely on each other. This moment of Quality Time is when you both feel most loved, cherished, and connected.

Why Quality Time Is the Most Important Love Language for Many

Emotional Connection: Quality Time fosters an unparalleled emotional connection by providing a dedicated space for open and meaningful interactions.

Feeling Valued: Being fully present with your partner conveys that they are valued and a top priority in your life.

Deep Understanding: It offers an opportunity for a deep understanding of each other's thoughts, feelings, and perspectives.

Building Memories: Quality Time creates lasting memories of moments shared together, strengthening the bond.

Reaffirming Commitment: Regular Quality Time reaffirms your commitment to the relationship and the love you share.

Make Time for Each Other Every Day

Picture this: It's the end of a long workday, and you're both exhausted. Instead of retreating to your separate corners of the house, you make an intentional choice to spend quality time together. You prepare a simple dinner, light some candles, and sit down at the dining table. As you savor your meal and converse, the stresses of the day melt away, and you're left with a sense of connection and togetherness.

Why Making Time for Each Other Every Day Matters

Consistent Connection: Daily Quality Time builds a consistent connection, ensuring that you stay emotionally engaged with each other.

Relationship Maintenance: It's a way of maintaining and nurturing the health of your relationship on a daily basis.

Preventing Drift: Regular Quality Time helps prevent emotional drift and keeps you closely connected.

Stress Reduction: Spending time together daily can be a source of stress relief and relaxation.

Creating Rituals: It allows you to create daily rituals that deepen your bond and create shared moments of joy.

How to Make Time for Each Other Every Day

Schedule It: Block out dedicated time in your daily schedule for Quality Time with your partner. Treat it as a non-negotiable appointment.

Prioritize: Make your partner a priority, even on the busiest days. Allocate time for them before other commitments.

Disconnect: Set boundaries with work, screens, and other distractions during your Quality Time. Be fully present.

Create Rituals: Establish daily rituals that involve your partner, such as cooking together, going for a walk, or sharing bedtime stories.

Unplug: Consider having phone-free or screen-free time to ensure that your focus is solely on each other.

Put Away Your Phones and Other Distractions

Imagine this: You and your partner are cuddled up on the couch, but there's a subtle but persistent distraction—the glow of your phones. You both decide to put your devices away, creating an intentional screen-free zone. As you do, you feel a shift in the atmosphere, a sense of being truly present with each other. Quality Time is about connecting heart to heart, and that requires leaving distractions behind.

Why Putting Away Distractions Is Essential

Undivided Attention: To truly connect during Quality Time, your attention should be undivided and focused on your partner.

Reducing Stress: Disconnecting from screens and other distractions can significantly reduce stress and mental clutter.

Deepening Conversation: A screen-free environment encourages deeper conversations and fosters active listening.

Enhancing Connection: Without distractions, you can better read your partner's emotions and connect on a more profound level.

Creating Boundaries: Setting boundaries with distractions shows your commitment to making Quality Time meaningful.

How to Put Away Distractions During Quality Time

Designate a Screen-Free Zone: Choose specific areas in your home where screens are not allowed during Quality Time.

Set Rules: Agree on ground rules for Quality Time, including turning off phones or setting them to silent mode.

Create Tech-Free Hours: Designate certain hours of the day or evening as tech-free, allowing you to connect without interruptions.

Use Do Not Disturb Mode: Activate the Do Not Disturb mode on your phones to minimize notifications during Quality Time.

Plan Tech-Free Activities: Engage in activities that naturally lend themselves to being screen-free, such as cooking, board games, or stargazing.

Quality Time is the language of presence, connection, and shared moments. It's a reminder that love thrives when we give it our undivided attention. As you journey through the chapters of your relationship, remember that Quality Time is the glue that holds you together, the canvas on which your shared memories are painted. So, dear reader, cherish the moments when you're truly present with your partner, invest in the quality of your time together, and let the bonds of love you create be a testament to the depth of your connection. Your love story is woven with threads of shared laughter, deep conversations, and the warmth of being fully present with each other. May your commitment to Quality Time continue to nurture and strengthen the beautiful tapestry of your relationship.

Chapter 13: Physical Touch

Welcome, dear reader, to a chapter that delves into the language of Physical Touch—the profound and often unspoken way we express love, affection, and intimacy. Physical touch is a universal language that transcends words, a gentle caress, a warm embrace, or a tender kiss can convey emotions that words alone cannot. In a world where touch can be both comforting and electrifying, we'll explore the art of physical connection and how it weaves a thread of love throughout our relationships.

Physical Touch Is a Powerful Way to Express Love and Affection

Imagine this: You and your partner are sitting on a quiet beach, the sun setting in the distance. As you watch the waves gently lap the shore, you reach for their hand and interlace your fingers. In that simple act of physical touch, you communicate love, comfort, and a deep sense of connection. It's a powerful way to express affection that goes beyond words.

Why Physical Touch Is a Powerful Expression of Love

Immediate Connection: Physical touch creates an immediate and intimate connection, allowing you to feel closer to your partner.

Emotional Communication: It's a form of emotional communication that can convey love, desire, comfort, and support.

Stress Reduction: Physical touch has the remarkable ability to reduce stress and anxiety, providing comfort in difficult moments.

Deepening Intimacy: It fosters a profound sense of intimacy and vulnerability that strengthens the emotional bond between partners.

Feeling Cherished: Being touched in a loving way can make us feel cherished and valued by our partner.

Be Mindful of Your Partner's Boundaries

Picture this: You and your partner are snuggled up on the couch, enjoying a movie night. Your partner has had a long day, and they're not in the mood for physical affection at the moment. You notice their body language and respect their boundaries by giving them space. Being mindful of your partner's boundaries is a crucial aspect of physical touch.

Why Being Mindful of Boundaries Is Important

Respect: It shows respect for your partner's autonomy and their comfort levels with physical touch.

Enhances Trust: Respecting boundaries enhances trust within the relationship, making your partner feel safe and secure.

Reduces Pressure: It reduces the pressure to engage in physical touch when one partner may not be in the mood, preventing discomfort or resentment.

Open Communication: Being mindful of boundaries encourages open communication about physical intimacy within the relationship.

Personal Space: Recognizing boundaries allows both partners to have personal space and control over their physical interactions.

How to Be Mindful of Your Partner's Boundaries

Communication: Have open and honest conversations with your partner about their boundaries and comfort levels regarding physical touch.

Observe Body Language: Pay attention to your partner's body language and cues to gauge their receptiveness to physical affection.

Ask for Consent: Always ask for consent before initiating physical touch, even if you've been together for a long time.

Respect Signals: If your partner communicates that they need space or are not in the mood for physical touch, respect their wishes without pressuring them.

Discuss Boundaries: Regularly revisit the topic of boundaries in your relationship to ensure that both partners feel heard and respected.

Don't Be Afraid to Initiate Physical Touch

Imagine this: You and your partner are getting ready for bed, and you decide to initiate physical touch by embracing them from behind and planting a gentle kiss on their neck. Your partner smiles and reciprocates, creating an intimate moment of connection. Initiating physical touch is an essential aspect of keeping the flame of intimacy alive.

Why Initiating Physical Touch Is Important

Demonstrates Desire: Initiating physical touch shows your desire and affection for your partner, reassuring them of your attraction.

Strengthens Connection: It strengthens the emotional bond between you and your partner, deepening your connection.

Balanced Effort: Initiating touch ensures that both partners share the responsibility of physical intimacy, creating a balanced dynamic.

Sensual Exploration: It allows you to explore and express your sensual desires within the relationship.

Keeps Passion Alive: Initiating physical touch helps keep the passion and excitement in your relationship alive and thriving.

How to Initiate Physical Touch

Start with Non-Verbal Cues: Use non-verbal cues such as prolonged eye contact, a flirtatious smile, or a light touch on the arm or shoulder.

Express Desire Verbally: Share your desires verbally by telling your partner how much you appreciate their physical presence or by expressing your affection verbally.

Be Spontaneous: Don't always wait for the "perfect" moment to initiate physical touch; sometimes, spontaneous gestures can be the most romantic.

Listen to Your Partner: Pay attention to your partner's responses and cues to ensure that they are receptive to your initiations.

Respect Boundaries: If your partner indicates that they're not in the mood for physical touch at that moment, respect their feelings and give them space.

Physical Touch is the language of closeness, comfort, and connection. It's a reminder that love is not just a word but a feeling that can be expressed through a gentle touch, a warm hug, or an affectionate kiss. As you continue to journey through the chapters of your relationship, let Physical Touch be the bridge that brings you closer, the language that conveys your deepest emotions, and the embrace that nurtures your bond. Your love story is a tapestry woven with threads of physical affection, creating a fabric of warmth, intimacy, and shared moments. May your commitment to Physical Touch continue to nurture the beautiful tapestry of your relationship, making it evermore vibrant and meaningful.

Chapter 14: The Five Love Languages in Action

Welcome to a chapter that showcases the real-life impact of the Five Love Languages in action. Throughout this journey, you've gained insights into Words of Affirmation, Acts of Service, Receiving Gifts, Quality Time, and Physical Touch. Now, it's time to witness the transformative power of these love languages in the lives of couples who have not just learned about them but have woven them into the very fabric of their relationships. These case studies serve as inspiring tales of love, growth, and connection.

Case Study 1: Sarah and Michael – Words of Affirmation

Sarah and Michael had been married for ten years when they began to feel a growing distance in their relationship. Work, kids, and the hustle and bustle of life had taken a toll on their emotional connection. They decided to take the Love Language quiz together and discovered that Sarah's primary love language was Words of Affirmation. For Michael, it was Acts of Service.

The Transformation:

Michael began to incorporate Words of Affirmation into their daily lives. He started leaving little notes of appreciation for Sarah, expressing his love and admiration. Instead of simply saying "I love you," he began to articulate why he loved her and what he cherished about her. The impact was almost immediate. Sarah felt seen and heard in a way she hadn't in years. She, in turn, started to appreciate Michael's Acts of Service even more, recognizing them as his way of showing love.

Sarah's Reflection: "The words Michael shares with me make me feel like the most important person in the world. It's not just about hearing

'I love you' but knowing why he loves me. It's brought us closer, and our love feels more vibrant than ever."

Case Study 2: Emily and David – Acts of Service

Emily and David were a couple in their thirties who had been together for five years. Their relationship was filled with love, but they had their fair share of conflicts. Emily was a busy attorney, and David worked long hours in IT. They realized that their love languages were mismatched—Emily's was Words of Affirmation, while David's was Acts of Service.

The Transformation:

Emily decided to learn more about Acts of Service, recognizing that David's way of expressing love was through actions. She started making an effort to cook meals together, help with chores, and even offer to take care of tasks that were typically David's responsibility. The change was palpable. David felt valued and supported in a way he hadn't before. In response, he began to use Words of Affirmation more often, expressing his love and appreciation.

David's Reflection: "Emily's acts of service made me feel like she truly cared about my well-being. It's not just about doing things for me but doing them together, which has brought us closer."

Case Study 3: Maria and Juan – Receiving Gifts

Maria and Juan were newlyweds who were deeply in love. However, they started to notice that they were drifting apart emotionally. They decided to take the Love Language quiz, and they discovered that Maria's primary love language was Receiving Gifts, while Juan's was Quality Time.

The Transformation:

Juan, initially puzzled by Maria's love language, made an effort to understand it better. He started giving her small, thoughtful gifts—a book she'd been wanting to read, a bouquet of her favorite flowers, or a handwritten note expressing his love. Maria felt cherished and loved with every gift. In response, she began to prioritize Quality Time with Juan. They started going on regular date nights and spending quality time together without distractions.

Maria's Reflection: "Juan's thoughtful gifts made me feel special and loved in a unique way. It's not about the gift's value but the thought and love behind it."

Case Study 4: Lily and Alex – Quality Time

Lily and Alex had been together for seven years. They were a couple who loved each other deeply but felt like they were stuck in a routine. After taking the Love Language quiz, they discovered that both of their primary love languages were Quality Time.

The Transformation:

Lily and Alex decided to make a deliberate effort to create more quality time together. They started by having regular "unplugged" evenings where they'd put away their phones and engage in activities they both enjoyed, such as cooking, playing board games, or stargazing. They also made it a point to have deep, meaningful conversations and share their dreams and goals. Their connection grew stronger, and they felt like they were falling in love all over again.

Alex's Reflection: "Quality Time isn't just about being physically present; it's about being emotionally present. Our decision to prioritize this love language brought back the spark in our relationship."

Case Study 5: Lisa and James – Physical Touch

Lisa and James were high school sweethearts who had been together for over a decade. They had a loving relationship but had recently experienced a dip in their emotional connection. After taking the Love Language quiz, they discovered that both of their primary love languages were Physical Touch.

The Transformation:

Lisa and James decided to reintroduce physical touch into their relationship in a more intentional way. They started by holding hands more often, hugging longer, and initiating more frequent physical affection. They also decided to prioritize cuddling and physical intimacy without the expectation of sex. These small changes reignited the spark in their relationship, and they felt more deeply connected than ever before.

Lisa's Reflection: "Physical Touch is like our secret language of love. It's not just about sex but about feeling close, connected, and cherished through physical affection."

These case studies illustrate the incredible impact of the Five Love Languages in real-life relationships. They show that love languages are not just theoretical concepts but practical tools that can rekindle and deepen the love between couples. By understanding each other's love languages and actively incorporating them into their daily lives, these couples were able to transform their relationships, reignite the spark of love, and strengthen their emotional connections. May these stories serve as an inspiration for you, dear reader, to explore and apply the power of the Five Love Languages in your own relationship journey. Your love story is unique, and by speaking the love languages that resonate with your partner, you can create a bond that is truly extraordinary.

Chapter 15: The Love Language and Conflict Resolution

Welcome, dear reader, to a chapter that explores the fascinating intersection of the Five Love Languages and conflict resolution within your relationship. Conflict is a natural part of any partnership, but how you navigate and resolve those conflicts can profoundly impact the health and longevity of your relationship. In this chapter, we'll delve into how understanding and applying the love languages can become a powerful tool in the art of resolving disputes, fostering understanding, and strengthening your bond even in times of disagreement.

How the Five Love Languages Can Help You Resolve Conflict in Your Relationship

Conflict often arises when there is a disconnect in the way partners communicate their love and emotional needs. This is where the Five Love Languages come into play—they provide a roadmap to understand and meet those needs more effectively. Here's how each love language can be applied to conflict resolution:

1. Words of Affirmation:

Express Appreciation During Conflict: Instead of focusing solely on the issue at hand, start by affirming your love for your partner. Express appreciation for their positive qualities and the efforts they make in the relationship. This sets a positive tone for the conversation.

Use Encouraging Language: Instead of using accusatory or blaming language, frame your concerns or complaints in an encouraging manner. For example, say, "I appreciate how hard you work, and I'd love for us to find a solution to this issue together."

2. Acts of Service:

Acts of Reconciliation: Use acts of service to demonstrate your commitment to resolving the conflict. Offering to help with tasks related to the issue at hand or taking on additional responsibilities can show your partner that you're dedicated to making things right.

Show Empathy: Acts of service can also be a way to express empathy. Preparing a meal or taking care of chores when your partner is upset or overwhelmed can convey your understanding and support.

3. Receiving Gifts:

Thoughtful Gestures: Consider using gifts as a way to make amends or express your desire to work through the conflict. A small, meaningful gift can symbolize your commitment to the relationship.

Apology Tokens: Sometimes, a tangible gesture can serve as an apology. It could be as simple as writing a heartfelt letter or giving a symbolic gift that signifies your remorse.

4. Quality Time:

Scheduled Conversations: If quality time is your partner's love language, schedule dedicated time to address the conflict. Create a safe, distraction-free space where you can have open and meaningful conversations.

Active Listening: During these quality time sessions, practice active listening. Give your partner your full attention, ask clarifying questions, and ensure they feel heard and valued.

5. Physical Touch:

Physical Reassurance: Physical touch can provide comfort during times of conflict. Holding hands, hugging, or sitting close to each other can convey your emotional support and reassurance.

Apology Through Touch: Physical touch can also be a way to apologize. A sincere hug or a gentle touch on the arm can communicate your remorse and desire to make amends.

Additional Tips for Conflict Resolution Using Love Languages:

Identify Your Partner's Love Language: Understand your partner's primary love language and keep it in mind during conflicts. Tailor your approach to address their emotional needs effectively.

Use Multiple Love Languages: While your partner may have a primary love language, they may also appreciate gestures in other languages. Be flexible and willing to utilize various love languages as needed.

Validate Feelings: Regardless of your approach, it's crucial to validate your partner's feelings and perspective during conflicts. Even if you don't agree, acknowledging their emotions fosters understanding.

Seek Compromise: Use the love languages as a tool for finding compromise. If, for example, your partner's love language is Acts of Service, and yours is Quality Time, you can compromise by setting aside quality time to work on a task together.

Apologize Sincerely: Apologizing is an essential part of conflict resolution. Ensure that your apology aligns with your partner's love language. If they value Words of Affirmation, a heartfelt apology letter might be more effective than a physical gesture.

Case Study: Sarah and Michael's Conflict Resolution Journey

Let's revisit the story of Sarah and Michael, whose primary love languages were Words of Affirmation and Acts of Service, respectively. One evening, they found themselves in a heated argument about the division of household chores. Sarah felt overwhelmed and unappreciated, while Michael felt that his efforts went unnoticed.

Conflict Resolution:

Sarah (Words of Affirmation): Instead of criticizing Michael, Sarah started the conversation by expressing her love and appreciation for him. She said, "I want you to know how much I love you and how grateful I am for all you do for us."

Michael (Acts of Service): Michael, in response, offered to take on some of the household chores that were causing Sarah stress. He said, "I want to make things easier for you. Let's work on a plan to share the responsibilities better."

Their understanding of each other's love languages allowed them to approach the conflict with empathy and appreciation. Sarah felt heard and valued, and Michael's acts of service demonstrated his commitment to their relationship. Through this process, they not only resolved the issue at hand but also grew closer.

Conflict is an inevitable part of any relationship, but it doesn't have to be detrimental. By understanding and applying the love languages, you can transform conflicts into opportunities for growth, understanding, and deeper connection. It's about speaking your partner's emotional language, showing empathy, and finding common ground even in moments of disagreement. Remember that conflicts are not signs of a failing relationship but opportunities to strengthen your bond by speaking the love languages of understanding, appreciation, and love.

Chapter 17: The Love Language and Long-Distance Relationships

Welcome, dear reader, to a chapter that explores the extraordinary world of long-distance relationships through the lens of the Five Love Languages. Love knows no boundaries, and in an age where physical distance is no longer a barrier to connection, understanding how to apply the love languages can be a lifeline that keeps your bond strong, your love burning bright, and your hearts close, even when you're miles apart.

How the Five Love Languages Can Help You Maintain a Strong Relationship Even When You're Apart

Long-distance relationships come with their unique set of challenges. The physical separation can make it challenging to convey love and maintain emotional closeness. This is where the Five Love Languages can be a beacon of light in the darkness, helping you bridge the gap and nurture your relationship from afar. Let's explore how each love language can be your ally in maintaining a strong long-distance relationship:

1. Words of Affirmation:

Frequent Communication: In a long-distance relationship, words become your primary mode of connection. Use words of affirmation to express your love, appreciation, and admiration. Send heartfelt texts, voice messages, or video calls to remind your partner of your affection.

Love Letters: Embrace the timeless tradition of love letters. Handwritten or digital, these letters allow you to pour your heart out and share your deepest feelings, fostering emotional intimacy.

2. Acts of Service:

Virtual Assistance: Acts of service can be adapted to the digital realm. Offer to help with tasks, even from afar. Whether it's troubleshooting tech issues, researching something for your partner, or coordinating surprise deliveries, these acts show your dedication.

Plan Virtual Dates: Acts of service can manifest in planning virtual dates or surprise experiences. Arrange an online cooking session, movie night, or even a surprise virtual trip to a place that holds sentimental value for both of you.

3. Receiving Gifts:

Thoughtful Online Shopping: Receiving gifts in a long-distance relationship can be a powerful way to feel connected. Use online shopping to send surprise gifts that reflect your partner's interests and tastes, reminding them of your love.

DIY Gifts: Get creative with DIY gifts that you can send through mail or digitally. Create personalized playlists, e-books, or even a digital scrapbook of your shared memories.

4. Quality Time:

Scheduled Virtual Dates: Quality time is all about being present with your partner. Schedule regular video calls where you can engage in meaningful conversations, share experiences, and simply enjoy each other's company.

Virtual Adventures: Quality time doesn't have to be static. Explore virtual tours, online games, or collaborative activities that allow you to create shared memories, even when you're physically apart.

5. Physical Touch:

Sensual Communication: Physical touch can be translated into sensual communication, even from a distance. Send messages that express your longing, affection, and desire for physical closeness. Use your words to create a sense of intimacy.

Virtual Intimacy: Explore ways to maintain physical intimacy through virtual means, such as sharing fantasies, intimate conversations, or even utilizing technology for remote physical connection, when both partners are comfortable with it.

Additional Tips for Maintaining a Strong Long-Distance Relationship Using Love Languages:

Know Each Other's Love Language: Understand your partner's primary love language and make an effort to speak it consistently, even from afar.

Scheduled Check-Ins: Establish a schedule for regular check-ins, whether it's daily texts, weekly video calls, or monthly visits, to maintain a sense of consistency and commitment.

Surprise Gestures: Surprise your partner with unexpected gestures that align with their love language. These surprises can serve as delightful reminders of your affection.

Communication Is Key: Open, honest, and transparent communication is the lifeblood of a long-distance relationship. Discuss your expectations, concerns, and goals openly.

Plan Future Visits: Work together to plan future visits or reunions. Having something to look forward to can provide a sense of hope and excitement.

Case Study: Emma and Liam's Long-Distance Love Story

Meet Emma and Liam, a couple who found themselves in a long-distance relationship due to work and family commitments. Emma's primary love language was Words of Affirmation, while Liam's was Quality Time. Their journey illustrates how the love languages became their guide in navigating the complexities of long-distance love.

Their Long-Distance Challenge:

Emma and Liam lived in different countries, making it challenging to be physically present for each other. Despite their deep love, they felt the emotional distance growing.

Application of Love Languages:

Emma (Words of Affirmation): Recognizing Liam's primary love language was Quality Time, Emma made an effort to express her love through heartfelt words and messages. She sent daily voice notes, telling Liam how much he meant to her, sharing her love, and expressing her longing to be together.

Liam (Quality Time): Liam, on the other hand, found creative ways to spend quality time together, despite the distance. They watched movies simultaneously while video chatting, played online games, and had virtual dinner dates. These shared experiences allowed them to feel closer.

The Result:

By focusing on each other's primary love languages, Emma and Liam were able to maintain their emotional connection. The love they expressed through words of affirmation and quality time bridged the physical gap. It wasn't always easy, but their dedication to understanding and applying the love languages kept their love alive and thriving.

Emma's Reflection: "Despite the distance, I felt more loved than ever because Liam spoke my love language through his words. It made me feel cherished and kept our connection strong."

Liam's Reflection: "Quality time became our lifeline. It wasn't about the quantity of time but the quality of our interactions. It made the distance feel less daunting."

Long-distance relationships, though challenging, can thrive when you understand and apply the Five Love Languages. Love is not limited by physical proximity; it transcends borders and knows no bounds. By speaking each other's love languages even when you're miles apart, you create a bridge that keeps your hearts connected. Embrace the power of words, acts of service, thoughtful gifts, quality time, and physical touch to nurture your love and build a relationship that not only survives but thrives in the face of distance. Your love story is a testament to the enduring strength of love, and with the love languages as your guide, you can create a bond that defies all odds.

Chapter 18: The Love Language and Blended Families

Welcome, dear reader, to a chapter that delves into the intricate world of blended families and how the Five Love Languages can be a guiding light in creating a loving and cohesive family unit. Blending families is a unique journey, filled with its own joys and challenges. In this chapter, we'll explore how understanding and applying the love languages can help you navigate this journey with compassion, communication, and love.

How the Five Love Languages Can Help You Create a Loving and Cohesive Blended Family

Blended families bring together individuals with diverse backgrounds, experiences, and expectations. It's a complex tapestry of emotions, where love, loyalty, and adaptation play pivotal roles. The Five Love Languages can serve as a vital tool in weaving this tapestry into a beautiful and harmonious family unit. Let's delve into how each love language can contribute to the success of a blended family:

1. Words of Affirmation:

Encourage Open Communication: Create an environment where family members feel comfortable expressing their thoughts and emotions. Use words of affirmation to acknowledge each other's feelings and experiences. Encourage open and honest conversations about the challenges and joys of blending families.

Individual Affirmation: Recognize that each family member may have different emotional needs. Tailor your words of affirmation to address these unique needs, ensuring that everyone feels valued and appreciated.

2. Acts of Service:

Support and Collaboration: Acts of service are a tangible way to show your commitment to the family. Collaborate on household chores, errands, and responsibilities, demonstrating your dedication to making the family thrive. Offer your assistance willingly and without expectation of praise.

Celebrate Milestones: Acts of service can be used to commemorate important family milestones, such as birthdays or anniversaries. Plan surprises or organize family activities that highlight the significance of these moments.

3. Receiving Gifts:

Symbolic Gestures: Gifts can symbolize the blending of hearts and lives in a blended family. Consider giving symbolic gifts that signify unity and acceptance. These gifts can be shared experiences, family mementos, or even custom-made items that reflect your unique family identity.

Individualized Thoughtfulness: When giving gifts, consider each family member's interests and preferences. Show that you've taken the time to understand their individuality and that you value their presence in the family.

4. Quality Time:

Family Rituals: Create family rituals that foster quality time together. Whether it's a weekly game night, Sunday brunch, or an annual family vacation, these rituals provide opportunities for bonding and shared experiences.

One-on-One Time: Recognize the importance of one-on-one time with each family member. Quality time can also involve spending time with stepchildren individually to build trust and nurture individual relationships.

5. Physical Touch:

Hugs and Affection: Physical touch is a powerful way to express love and comfort in a blended family. Offer hugs, pats on the back, or a comforting touch during difficult moments. These gestures convey a sense of belonging and security.

Reinforce Boundaries: Be mindful of physical touch boundaries, especially when integrating new family members. Respect individual preferences and comfort levels to ensure that everyone feels safe and valued.

Additional Tips for Building a Loving and Cohesive Blended Family Using Love Languages:

Family Meetings: Hold regular family meetings where each member has a chance to express their feelings, concerns, and joys. Use this time to discuss family goals, expectations, and plans.

Respect Individual Identities: Acknowledge and respect the individual identities of family members. Celebrate their unique backgrounds, interests, and experiences.

Blend Traditions: Blend family traditions and customs from each household to create new traditions that honor the past while embracing the future.

Seek Professional Guidance: Consider family counseling or therapy to address any complex issues or conflicts that may arise during the blending process.

Patience and Flexibility: Understand that blending families takes time. Be patient and flexible, allowing each family member to adjust at their own pace.

Case Study: The Rodriguez-Jones Blended Family

Meet the Rodriguez-Jones family, a loving and diverse blended family that beautifully illustrates how the love languages can create harmony and love in a blended family setting. The family consists of Maria and David, who each brought two children from previous marriages into their union.

The Blending Challenge:

When Maria and David first merged their families, they faced the challenge of integrating their children, who ranged in age from 8 to 15. The children had different personalities, interests, and expectations.

Application of Love Languages:

Words of Affirmation: Maria and David regularly expressed words of affirmation to all the children, individually and as a group. They encouraged open communication and provided a safe space for the children to share their thoughts and feelings about the blending process.

Acts of Service: The couple made acts of service a family affair. They involved the children in planning and executing acts of service for each other and the community. This created a sense of unity and responsibility among the children.

Receiving Gifts: To symbolize their unity, the family started a tradition of exchanging meaningful gifts during special occasions and family milestones. These gifts were carefully chosen to reflect the family's shared experiences and values.

Quality Time: The Rodriguez-Jones family prioritized quality time together. They established weekly family game nights, movie nights, and outdoor adventures. This allowed the children to bond and create lasting memories.

Physical Touch: Physical touch was used to create a sense of comfort and belonging in the family. Hugs, high-fives, and even playful wrestling matches were common expressions of affection.

The Result:

Through their dedication to applying the love languages, the Rodriguez-Jones family successfully blended their diverse backgrounds and created a loving and cohesive family unit. The children not only formed strong sibling bonds but also developed deep connections with their step-parents. The love languages became the family's shared language of love and understanding.

Maria's Reflection: "We wanted our family to be a place where each child felt cherished, respected, and loved for who they are. The love languages helped us bridge any gaps and create a home filled with love."

David's Reflection: "Blending our family wasn't always easy, but seeing our children grow into a close-knit, loving group makes it all worth it. The love languages were our guiding light."

Blending families is a journey of love, adaptation, and unity. With the Five Love Languages as your compass, you can navigate this journey with compassion and create a loving and cohesive blended family. Embrace words of affirmation, acts of service, thoughtful gifts, quality time, and physical touch as your tools to nurture bonds, build understanding, and foster love among all family members. Remember that every step you take in applying the love languages brings you closer to a harmonious and loving blended family that cherishes the uniqueness of each member and celebrates the strength of unity.

Chapter 19: The Love Language and Infidelity

Welcome, dear reader, to a chapter that delves into the delicate and often painful topic of infidelity within a relationship. Infidelity is a profound breach of trust, one that can leave emotional scars and fractures in even the most robust partnerships. However, this chapter is not solely about the act of infidelity itself, but rather, how understanding and applying the Five Love Languages can play a pivotal role in healing from infidelity and rebuilding a stronger, more resilient relationship.

How the Five Love Languages Can Help You Heal from Infidelity and Rebuild Your Relationship

Infidelity shatters the very foundation of trust in a relationship, leaving both partners in a state of emotional turmoil. The journey to healing is challenging, but it's not insurmountable. Understanding and applying the love languages can be a path towards reconciliation and rebuilding trust. Let's explore how each love language can contribute to the healing process:

1. Words of Affirmation:

Apology and Acknowledgment: If you've been unfaithful, it's essential to offer a sincere and heartfelt apology to your partner. Use words of affirmation to express your remorse, acknowledge the pain you've caused, and convey your commitment to rebuilding trust.

Validation of Feelings: Understand that your partner may need words of affirmation to process their emotions. Validate their feelings of hurt, anger, and betrayal. Let them know that you are willing to listen and understand their perspective.

2. Acts of Service:

Rebuilding Through Action: Acts of service can be a way to rebuild trust. Show your commitment to change and regain your partner's trust by taking on responsibilities, being consistent in your actions, and fulfilling promises.

Reparative Acts: Consider acts of service as a way to make amends. Whether it's attending couples therapy, seeking counseling individually, or initiating conversations about the future, take proactive steps to repair the relationship.

3. Receiving Gifts:

Symbolic Gestures: Consider using gifts as symbolic gestures of your commitment to the relationship. These gifts can symbolize your willingness to make amends and rebuild trust. Be thoughtful in your gift choices to convey your sincerity.

Anniversary of Renewal: Choose a meaningful date to commemorate your commitment to rebuilding the relationship. Exchange gifts that symbolize your shared journey towards healing and reconnection.

4. Quality Time:

Focused Conversations: Quality time is essential for open and honest communication. Dedicate time to have focused conversations about the issues surrounding infidelity. Allow your partner to express their feelings and concerns while actively listening.

Rekindling Connection: Use quality time to rekindle your emotional connection. Engage in activities that you both enjoy, reminisce about positive memories, and rediscover shared interests.

5. Physical Touch:

Reestablishing Intimacy: Physical touch can play a crucial role in rebuilding emotional and physical intimacy. Engage in non-sexual physical touch, such as hugs, handholding, or cuddling, to foster a sense of closeness and safety.

Rebuilding Trust: Re-establishing physical touch should be a gradual and consensual process. Respect your partner's boundaries and consent at all times to rebuild trust and ensure emotional safety.

Additional Tips for Healing from Infidelity Using Love Languages:

Transparent Communication: Maintain open and honest communication throughout the healing process. Both partners should feel safe expressing their thoughts, concerns, and needs.

Seek Professional Help: Consider couples therapy or counseling to navigate the complexities of healing from infidelity. A trained therapist can provide guidance and facilitate productive conversations.

Patience and Empathy: Healing takes time. Be patient with each other's emotions and progress. Practice empathy and understanding, recognizing that both partners are on a journey toward healing.

Rebuilding Trust: Rebuilding trust is a gradual process. Make consistent efforts to rebuild trust through your actions and words.

Forgiveness: Forgiveness is a significant component of healing. Both partners may need to work on forgiveness, whether it's forgiving the person who strayed or forgiving oneself for any role played in the infidelity.

Case Study: Sarah and John's Journey of Healing

Sarah and John had been married for ten years when Sarah discovered John's infidelity. The discovery was devastating, and their relationship seemed irreparably broken. However, their commitment to understanding and applying the love languages became a turning point in their journey of healing.

The Healing Process:

Words of Affirmation: John initiated open and heartfelt conversations, using words of affirmation to express his remorse and commitment to their relationship. He acknowledged the pain he had caused and validated Sarah's emotions.

Acts of Service: John took proactive steps to make amends. He offered to attend individual therapy to address the underlying issues that led to his infidelity. These actions demonstrated his commitment to change.

Receiving Gifts: To symbolize their renewed commitment, Sarah and John exchanged meaningful gifts on their anniversary. The gifts represented their journey of healing and rebuilding trust.

Quality Time: The couple dedicated time to quality conversations, both in therapy and at home. They focused on rebuilding their emotional connection and rediscovering the love they once shared.

Physical Touch: Physical touch played a crucial role in reestablishing intimacy. They initiated non-sexual physical touch as a way to rebuild trust and emotional closeness.

The Result:

Through their commitment to understanding and applying the love languages, Sarah and John embarked on a journey of healing and reconciliation. While their relationship faced challenges, they ultimately emerged stronger and more connected than before. Their story is a testament to the power of love, forgiveness, and the love languages in mending the deepest of wounds.

Sarah's Reflection: "The love languages allowed us to communicate our needs and feelings in a way that felt safe and understood. It gave us a framework for rebuilding our relationship."

John's Reflection: "Healing from infidelity was the most challenging thing we've ever faced, but it also brought us closer. The love languages helped us find our way back to each other."

Infidelity is undoubtedly one of the most painful experiences a relationship can endure. However, with dedication, open communication, and the application of the Five Love Languages, healing and rebuilding trust are possible. These love languages offer a roadmap for expressing remorse, fostering understanding, and rekindling the love that initially brought you together. Remember that healing takes time and patience, but with love as your guiding light, you can emerge from this challenging journey with a stronger and more resilient relationship.

Chapter 20: The Love Language and the Future

Dear reader, as we journey towards the conclusion of this book, we find ourselves at a crossroads, looking both backward at the wisdom we've uncovered and forward to the endless possibilities that the Five Love Languages hold for our relationships and the world at large. In this final chapter, we explore the future of the love languages and how they can continue to guide and transform our lives.

The Future of the Five Love Languages

The Five Love Languages, originally introduced by Dr. Gary Chapman, have proven to be a timeless and invaluable resource for understanding and improving our relationships. But what does the future hold for these love languages?

1. Evolution and Expansion:

The love languages have evolved over the years to encompass various aspects of human connection. As our understanding of relationships deepens, we can expect the love languages to continue expanding and adapting to meet the needs of diverse relationships, including LGBTQ+ partnerships, non-traditional families, and more.

2. Integration with Technology:

In the digital age, technology has transformed the way we connect with one another. We can anticipate the integration of the love languages into relationship-focused apps, online therapy, and virtual relationship tools that enhance our ability to communicate love and appreciation in the digital realm.

3. Cross-Cultural Relevance:

As the world becomes more interconnected, the love languages will play a vital role in fostering cross-cultural understanding and empathy. They offer a universal language of love that transcends cultural boundaries and can bridge gaps in international relationships.

4. Enhanced Education:

Education on the love languages will become more widely accessible. We can expect to see educational institutions, therapists, and relationship experts incorporating the love languages into their curricula and therapeutic approaches, ensuring that individuals are equipped with the tools to build healthier relationships from a young age.

How the Five Love Languages Can Continue to Help People Build Stronger Relationships

The enduring relevance of the Five Love Languages lies in their ability to provide practical guidance for building and nurturing relationships. Here's how they can continue to make a difference in our lives:

1. Communication Mastery:

The love languages offer a framework for effective communication in relationships. By understanding each other's love languages, individuals can communicate their feelings and needs more clearly, reducing misunderstandings and conflicts.

2. Emotional Resilience:

Understanding and applying the love languages can enhance emotional resilience. They help individuals express love and support during challenging times, reinforcing the bonds that help us weather life's storms.

3. Relationship Sustainability:

The love languages provide essential tools for maintaining long-term relationships. By speaking each other's love languages consistently, couples can keep the flame of love burning and strengthen their bonds over time.

4. Healing and Recovery:

In times of crisis or difficulty, the love languages offer a path to healing and recovery. They enable individuals and couples to rebuild trust, nurture emotional intimacy, and find their way back to a place of love and understanding.

5. Building Bridges:

The love languages can help build bridges between individuals with different backgrounds, perspectives, and experiences. They offer a common language of love that fosters empathy, understanding, and connection.

6. Creating Healthy Families:

Teaching the love languages to future generations can contribute to the creation of healthier families and relationships. By understanding and speaking the love languages, parents can create an environment of love and support for their children.

7. Nurturing Self-Love:

The love languages also apply to self-love and self-care. Individuals can learn to recognize and meet their own emotional needs, leading to increased self-esteem and personal growth.

As we conclude our journey through the world of the Five Love Languages, we want to express our heartfelt gratitude for embarking on this exploration with us. The love languages have the power to transform relationships, heal wounds, and create lasting bonds of love and understanding.

But remember, dear reader, that the journey of love is ongoing. The love languages provide a roadmap, but it is you who must take the steps. Love is not a destination; it is the journey itself—the daily choices, the heartfelt conversations, and the small acts of love that make life rich and meaningful.

In the end, it is the love we give and receive that defines us. It is the love we share with our partners, our families, and our friends that lights up our world. As you continue on your journey of love, may the Five Love Languages be your guiding star, illuminating the path to deeper connections, stronger relationships, and a life filled with love.

Thank you for joining us on this remarkable journey, and may your future be filled with love in all its beautiful languages.

Don't miss out!

Visit the website below and you can sign up to receive emails whenever SERGIO RIJO publishes a new book. There's no charge and no obligation.

https://books2read.com/r/B-A-COYW-FLBOC

BOOKS 2 READ

Connecting independent readers to independent writers.

Did you love *The Love Language: How to Speak Your Partner's Love Language and Build a Deeper Connection*? Then you should read *Inner Child Healing: The Key to Overcoming Negative Beliefs, Self-Sabotage, and Unlocking Your True Potential*[1] by SERGIO RIJO!

Are you tired of feeling stuck in negative patterns and behaviors? Do you struggle with self-sabotage and limiting beliefs that hold you back from reaching your goals? Inner Child Healing is the key to unlocking your true potential and creating a fulfilling life.

In this powerful book, I guide you through the process of healing your inner child, uncovering the root causes of negative beliefs and behaviors, and creating a new, positive mindset. With practical exercises, real-life examples, and a compassionate, supportive tone,

1. https://books2read.com/u/4DJvpD

2. https://books2read.com/u/4DJvpD

Inner Child Healing empowers you to break free from the past and create a brighter future.

You'll learn how to:

Identify and heal childhood wounds that are holding you backOvercome self-sabotage and limiting beliefsBuild healthy relationships and set boundariesPractice self-care and cultivate a positive mindsetUse gratitude and mindfulness to stay focused on the presentInner Child Healing is not just a book, it's a journey of self-discovery and growth. Whether you're just beginning your healing journey or you're looking for new tools to deepen your practice, this book is for you. With Inner Child Healing, you'll discover the power of healing your inner child and unlocking your true potential.

Also by SERGIO RIJO

Breaking Free: A Guide to Recovery from Narcissistic Abuse
Dreamweaving: The Ultimate Guide to Entering Someone's Dreams
From Isolation to Balance: The Ultimate Guide to Remote Work
Success
The Twin Flames Blueprint: A Guide to Achieving Union and
Embracing the Journey
Insta-Profit: 25 Proven Ways to Monetize Your Instagram Presence
The Awakening: Archangel Michael's Message for a Unified and
Evolved Humanity
Unlock Your Potential: 10 Key Skills for Young People to Have
Success in Life and Career
30 Days of Spiritual Transformation: How to Change Your Life
Through the Power of Spirituality
Brain Overhaul: Upgrading Your Mind for Accelerated Learning and
Success
30 Days to a Richer You: The Millionaire Success Habits That Will
Change Your Life
Separate but Connected: A Guide to Navigating the Twin Flame
Separation Stage
The Rise of AI Income: Using Artificial Intelligence for Financial
Success
Anime Tattoo Design Book: 300+ Designs for Fans and Tattoo
Artists
The Art of Butterfly Tattoos: 300+ Designs to Inspire Your Next
Tattoo

Living with Purpose: Finding Meaning and Direction in Life

Breaking Free from Self-Sabotage: Overcoming Destructive Patterns and Achieving Your Goals

Uncovering the Shadows: A Journey through Shadow Work

The Science of Nutrition for Athletes: Understanding the Specific Nutritional Needs of Athletes for Optimal Performance and Recovery

The Magic of Saying No: How to Establish Boundaries and Take Charge of Your Life

Connecting with the Divine: Tools and Techniques for Powerful Prayer

Living in Harmony: The Complete Guide to Permaculture and Sustainable Living

Angelic Assistance: How to Connect with Your Guardian Angels and Spirit Guides for Support

Beyond Belief: Unraveling the Psychology of Ghosts and Hauntings

Transform Your Health with Intermittent Fasting: A Comprehensive Guide to Techniques and Benefits

Discover the Secrets of Lucid Dreaming: How to Use Your Dreams to Transform Your Life

Existential Crisis: Strategies for Finding Hope and Renewal in Life's Darkest Moments

The 12 Spiritual Laws of the Universe: A Comprehensive Guide to Achieving Personal Growth and Spiritual Enlightenment

The 144,000 Lightworkers: Healing and Awakening Humanity to Save the World

Defying Age: The Ultimate Guide to Living a Long and Healthy Life

Unlocking the Secrets of Astral Projection: Techniques for Successful Out-of-Body Experiences

Inner Child Healing: The Key to Overcoming Negative Beliefs, Self-Sabotage, and Unlocking Your True Potential

Raising Your Vibration: A Holistic Guide to Achieving Emotional and Spiritual Well-being

Psychic Vampires and Empaths: The Ultimate Guide to Protection and Healing with Energy, Crystals, Reiki, and More

Developing Clairvoyance: The Ultimate Guide to Unlocking Your Psychic Gifts and Connecting with the Spiritual World

Mastering Telekinesis: A Step-by-Step Guide to Developing Your Psychokinetic Abilities

Afterlife: Understanding Signs and Communication from Deceased Loved Ones

Navigating Spiritual Depression: Finding Meaning in the Dark Night of the Soul

Journey of the Old Soul: Navigating Life with Empathy, Wisdom, and Purpose

Third Eye Awakening: A Comprehensive Guide to Unlocking Your Inner Vision, Enhancing Intuition, and Activating the Pineal Gland for Spiritual Insight and Heightened Perception

Telepathy Unveiled: A Journey into the Secrets of Sending Telepathic Messages and Psychic Development

44 Letters from God: Divine Guidance for Life's Journey

Mastering Emotional Intelligence: Strategies for Cultivating Self-Awareness, Self-Regulation, and Empathy

The Power of Solitude: Embracing Alone Time for Self-Discovery and Fulfillment

The Ultimate Guide to Beekeeping: Tips and Tricks for Beginners

Akashic Records and Past Lives: Understanding How Past Lives Can Impact Your Present and Future

Mindful Eating for Emotional Freedom: Break the Cycle of Emotional Eating Habits

Stand-Up Comedy: A Guide to Writing and Performing with Confidence

The Art of Budget Travel: Techniques for Saving Money and Maximizing Experiences While Traveling

The Mystic Art of Alchemy: Understanding the Symbolism and Practice of Spiritual Transformation

The Power Within: A Guide to Self-Healing with Energy

Solo Travel: Techniques for Planning and Executing a Successful Solo Trip

The Art of Extreme Budgeting: How to Live on Almost Nothing and Thrive

The Science of Luck: How to Increase Your Odds of Success

The Science of Color: Understanding the Psychology of Color

The Secret Life of the Brain: Exploring the Mysteries and Wonders of Our Most Vital Organ

Listen Up: Unlocking the Secrets of Active Listening

The Power of Self-Love: Transforming Your Life Through Compassion and Acceptance

The Science of Time Travel: Theories and Possibilities Explained

Beyond the Mind's Illusions: Mastering Thought Patterns for Freedom from Suffering

Quantum Light Mastery: Unleashing Infinite Power

The Archetype Code: Unveiling Your True Self

The Empath's Path: Journey to Self-Discovery

Surrender to Freedom: Letting Go for Conscious Living

Metabolism Unleashed: Unlocking Your Body's Hidden Weight Loss Potential

Unburdened: Liberating Your True Self from Emotionally Immature Parents

Healing the Unseen Wounds: Unlocking the Power of Resilience

The Wild Within: Embracing Discomfort for Health, Growth, and Happiness

Beyond the Ordinary: Unleashing Your Supernatural Potential

The Pendulum Power Guide: Unleash Magic, Healing, and Divination in Your Life

Beyond the Veil: Unleashing Your Spiritual Mediumship

Awakening the Shaman Within: Unveiling the Mysteries of Ancient Wisdom

The Sacred Geometry Guidebook: Illuminating the Power of Patterns

Law of Attraction Mastery: Unleashing Your Manifestation Power for Abundance and Fulfillment

Cosmic Harmony: A Guide to Unraveling Synchronicities, Signs, and Spiritual Awakening for a Fulfilling Life

Journey to the Ancestral Realms: Unveiling the Secrets of Spirit Guides

Whispers of Eternity: Exploring the Mysteries of Death, Reincarnation, and the Afterlife

Starseed Secrets: Unveiling Your Cosmic DNA

The Joyful Mindset Makeover: Transform Your Life Through Positive Emotions

Mastering Emotional Resilience: Thriving in the Face of Challenges

Uncomplicate: Mastering Happiness and Success Through Simplicity

Success Habits: Unveiling the Blueprint to Achievement and Fulfillment

Unleash Your Creative Genius: Tapping into Your Innate Imagination and Innovation

Beyond Materialism: Finding Meaning and Happiness in a Consumerist World

Redefining Success: Creating a Life Aligned with Your Values and Purpose

Living Beyond Limits: Unleashing Your Full Potential through Spiritual Laws

The Enlightened Mindset: Cultivating Spiritual Awareness in Everyday Life

The Path to Inner Harmony: Balancing Spiritual Enlightenment and Modern Living

Empowered Intuition: A Guide to Navigating Life through Spiritual Insight

Manifesting Miracles: Activating Spiritual Laws to Create Your Dream Life

Sacred Relationships: Nurturing Connections through Spiritual Laws

The Soulful Entrepreneur: Integrating Spiritual Laws into Business Success

Interpreting the Signs: A Guide to Understanding Messages from the Spirit World

Mystical Synchronicities: Exploring the Divine Order in Everyday Life

The Minimalist Vegan: How to Live a More Ethical, Eco-Friendly, and Healthier Life

The Love Language: How to Speak Your Partner's Love Language and Build a Deeper Connection

The Power of Focus: How to Stay Focused on Your Goals and Achieve Success

About the Author

Join me on an adventure through captivating stories! I'm Sergio Rijo, a passionate writer with 20 years of experience in crafting books across genres. Let's explore new worlds together and get hooked from start to finish.

Printed by Libri Plureos GmbH in Hamburg, Germany